A KITCHEN WELL-TRAVELLED

SAI YOGANATHAN

ACKNOWLEDGEMENTS

This book would not have been possible without the support and encouragement of my loving husband, Yoga, my adorable children, Pranavan and Varayini, my daughter-in-law, Tamera and son-in-law, Prasanna. Thank you for coaching me and tirelessly helping me with the artwork and strategic decisions. You guys are the best mentors and your constructive criticism helped me to lift the standard and quality of photography and design of this book.

Tamera, special thanks for the superb brand name selection. Varayini, thank you for seeding the idea of a cookbook and inspiring me to publish. Both of you girls are amazing!

I wish to thank my mother, Jeeva, for showing me the fundamentals of cooking and supporting my culinary adventures. Words cannot express my gratitude to my late father, my late grandparents, and my extended family for their unconditional love and nurturing my desire to cook.

Special thanks to my loving sisters, Aneetha and Ramani, for directing me to the kitchen during school holidays to prepare snacks and cakes to satisfy your mid-afternoon cravings. I truly value your supervision and critiques.

Rod and Mirani, thank you both for joining me in the journey and for kindly writing the foreword for this book.

Many thanks to all my friends for boosting my confidence, making me feel like a 'master chef' and urging me to publish this book.

Deborah Shaw, thank you for your professional advice and assistance with this manuscript. My heartiest thanks to my niece Brindha and nephew Krishna for their critiques and review of the final document.

And lastly, a very special thanks to Karen McKenzie for voluntarily helping me with some of the fundamental decisions involved with publishing.

FOREWORD

Adopting so many countries as home has left Sai with a breadth of knowledge, honed taste, and the ability to integrate traditional foods into new environments. Until this book came to being, I thought her spice blends were family secrets but I've now seen how she meticulously and systematically experiments and refines her blends.

Sai's exposure to flavour, as well as her reflection on it, make her invitations to dine unmissable. When I sit at Sai's table, I expect something from Sri Lanka, but with a local twist because many of the fresh Sri Lankan ingredients cannot be found in New Zealand. What ingredients can be collected, usually fresh from the local market, provide an angle on these dishes unique to New Zealand. The breadth of recipes attests to her knowledge of available foods, but also to her knowledge of contemporary New Zealand food.

Her short eats vary from the traditional to contemporary and I would recommend the beautifully contrasting sweetness and saltiness of seeni sambal and goat's cheese. But it is the meat, fish and vegetable dishes that I get most excited about. Take for example, the Zimbabwe chicken with its beautifully mellow, integrated flavours from capsicums and black pepper. She is not hesitant to bring in umami flavours in her wonderfully balanced panko crusted fish and miso broth, or to use quinoa in her Super Puttu. And of course I must mention the desserts – the mango pudding is my favourite for its smoothness and visual appeal. Some dishes are not without their technical challenges but do try the traditional Sri Lankan egg hoppers and serve with the seeni sambal.

The fact is, Sai's cooking is so far from traditional, and so uniquely her. I am glad to see her meals in a recipe book, where the recipes will be passed on to countless others and will make it possible for anyone to reap the benefits of Sai's culinary experiments.

I can recommend all these dishes as I know the dedication and love that has gone into their creation.

Dr Rod Keillor
Owner of Black Quail Estate Vineyard & Fellow Foodie

010 Introduction

018 Key

021 Shopping + ingredients

033 Spice blends

043 Staples/basics

060 Short eats/savoury bites

097 Meat

CONTENTS

128 Seafood

169 Salads + veges

197 Curries

234 Meat-free curries

267 Sambals, pickles + relishes

287 Sweet treats

357 Dinner party menus

384 Index

HELLO, I'M SAI

I was born in Jaffna, a peninsula in the northern province of Sri Lanka. This book is my ultimate recipe collection and it showcases my family traditions, childhood memories, culinary adventures and travel experiences. I began my gastronomic journey in Sri Lanka and added many recipes to my repertoire during my tenures in Africa, New Zealand and Australia.

My cooking style embraces traditional techniques and exotic spices from my motherland, whilst combining these with modern elements inspired by different cuisines I have relished around the world.

One of the greatest pleasures in my life is cooking and sharing food with family and friends. My love of cooking, food, and the art of entertaining prompted me to compile and share the very best recipes from my collection with you.

My food is all about quality ingredients, fresh produce, craftsmanship, experimentation, and entertainment – and lots of passion.

ME AND MY YOUNGER SISTER

MY MOTHER, AUNTIES AND COUSIN

I began assisting my mother in the kitchen from a young age. Over the years, she nurtured me and gave me the courage to explore different ingredients and flavours. She taught me that there are no hard and fast rules to cooking. Her advice gave me the confidence and courage to experiment with different ingredients and flavours across a variety of cuisines.

I recall speaking to my mother about writing a cookbook and she welcomed my aspirations. She recollected that my auntie, Ariamalar, had plans to publish a cookbook a long time ago. My aunt had a devotion to cooking and entertained her delighted guests with fabulous flair, presenting delectable four-course meals. Sadly, she passed away before she had the opportunity to realise her lifelong wish. This grounded me in the realisation that one should not hesitate to follow one's dreams. I was inspired to see this publication through to completion.

Food is to be enjoyed by everyone, and it all comes down to what works best for you and your family. I hope this book inspires you to create your very own cooking memories to share with your loved ones. With a few exceptions, almost every spice called for in my recipes is readily available in supermarkets. Give yourself some time. Experiment with the ingredients on hand to unleash the champion chef within you!

To find out more about food safety, check out Food Standards Australia New Zealand at www.foodstandards.gov.au

MY OLD RECIPE BOOK, FILLED WITH HANDWRITTEN RECIPES FROM MY MOTHER.

I TREASURE MY MOTHER'S ORIGINAL RECIPES.

1 tsp. Ginger + Garlic
2 sprigs curry leaves
6 small potatoes
500 ml. water
Chopped Dhania

Heat oil, fry one

This is my late father Rajnedram was an engineer who worked in Sri Lanka and Africa. He was also a food lover who liked to travel and had a great interest in fine arts and culture. He suffered a brain tumour and passed away shortly after I was married. I am donating 100% of my profits from this book to the New Zealand Brain Tumour Trust. To find out more, go to www.nzbtt.com

KEY

These days cooking a delicious, healthy meal and keeping everyone happy can be an arduous task. Some of the guess work has been taken out with this visual guide to diets and additional information that accompanies each recipe. Please use your best judgement regarding dietary requirements or allergies of others.

Gary Paterson has a degree in Biochemistry and Human Physiology as well as a Diploma in Brewing from the Siebel Institute of Brewing in Chicago. He was a brewer at DB Breweries for 16 years and for the past 27 years has been a contractor to the brewing industry. He has designed and manufactured 19 breweries – in New Zealand, Tahiti, Samoa, China and Japan.

Point Wines is a boutique wine cellar in Northcote Point, a stone's throw from Auckland city. Established in 1996, they specialise in New Zealand wines, including small boutique producers you can't find in supermarkets. They like to support smaller ventures of passionate people like themselves. They also sell wines from around the world. Inspired by their travels in Europe and the USA, in 2009 owners Simon and Jacquie launched Stafford Road Wine Bar next door. They believe great wine should be shared and paired with great food and vice versa.

I LOVE TO COOK WITH THE FRESHEST AND FINEST INGREDIENTS THAT EACH SEASON HAS TO OFFER. NO MATTER WHICH PART OF THE WORLD I'M IN, I LIKE VISITING FRESH FOOD AND FARMERS MARKETS. ALTHOUGH I HAVE LIVED IN MULTIPLE COUNTRIES AND TRAVELLED THE WORLD, I CAN'T SHAKE THE FEELING THAT THE PRODUCE DOWNUNDER JUST TASTES BETTER!

SHOPPING + INGREDIENTS

INGREDIENTS

Below is a list of favourite ingredients that I commonly use, some of which may be unfamilar to you.

Asafoetida is a strong, pungent spice which is used in Indian cuisine. It is available in powder or solid forms and is one of the main ingredients required in the preparation of sambar, a popular lentil vegetable soup. It is usually available in the ethnic section of most of the supermarket chains these days.

Cardamom pods have a powerful but delightfully sweet aroma. The outer husk surrounds the black cardamom seeds which are the main spice. Used in Indian and Sri Lankan cooking, cardamom is also commonly used in Arabic and Persian cuisines to flavour both savoury and sweet dishes.

Chana dal is a small variety of chickpea that has been split and polished. Not only is it delicious, it is also very nutritious and one of the most popular legumes used in Indian cooking. In powdered form, chana dal is referred to as besan or chickpea flour, and has a myriad of culinary uses.

Chermoula spice is a lovely, traditional spice blend used in Moroccan and Tunisian cooking. There are many different recipes for this spice and the proportions vary widely. But the most common ingredients are garlic, coriander, lemon, paprika and cumin.

Cinnamon comes from the inner bark of the cinnamon tree which is native to Sri Lanka. The bark is dried and rolled into quills, which have a pleasing, delicate aroma and refined taste. There are a few different types of cinnamon available in the market. The most common is Cassia, a strong-smelling bark which is hard and dark in colour. Look for the spice labelled Ceylon or Sri Lankan cinnamon.

Coconut is known for its versatility and is often used in curries and sambal in Sri Lanka. Freshly grated, chipped, desiccated, milk, cream, water, or flour, coconut comes in various forms these days.

Curry leaves are greatly valued as a flavouring agent in Sri Lankan and Indian cooking. Fresh leaves release a strong aroma when bruised and are used to enhance the flavour and piquancy of many dishes. The aroma of dried leaves is considerably less.

Curry powder (Jaffna style) is an essential ingredient in Sri Lankan cooking. Jaffna style curry powder is traditionally prepared with premium quality ingredients measured to precise proportions, dry roasted and then milled in a commercial grinding mill. Jaffna curry powder is chilli based and it presents the most incredible, exotic flavour in curries. There are various curry powders available on the market but King's curry powder is one of the best brands. You will find it in most Sri Lankan grocery stores.

Dried fish has a strong flavour as a result of the curing process but has several years' shelf life. Salting with open air drying is one of the preservation methods used in Sri Lanka. Maldive fish, dried anchovies/sprats and Karuvadu (dried fish pieces) are some of the traditional dried fish varieties that are a fundamental ingredient in Sri Lankan cuisine.

Gelatine is used mainly as a setting agent. It comes in various forms. Powdered gelatine is familiar to home cooks whereas gelatine leaves/sheets are commonly used in commercial kitchens. I find gelatine leaves provide smooth, clearer results.

Harissa is a flavoursome Tunisian blend of spices that can be used as a marinade or to flavour couscous, seafood, meat or vegetarian dishes. It comes in a powdered form or as a paste preserved in olive oil.

Jaggery is a dark-coloured unrefined sugar made from sugar cane juice and used as a sweetener. Palm sugar is also an acceptable substitute.

Kashmiri chilli powder imparts a vibrant red colour to a dish without making it too spicy. Available at most Indian and Sri Lankan grocery stores or large supermarkets.

Miso is a traditional Japanese paste produced with fermented soybeans. It is used for sauces and flavouring vegetables, meat or seafood. Instant miso soup varieties and miso paste are available from most supermarkets.

Nigella seeds are also known as black onion seeds or kalonji spice. These seeds look very similar to black sesame seeds but have an the scent of oregano when bruised. They are commonly used in Indian cuisine to flavour pickles and seafood dishes.

Pandan leaf is a primary ingredient used as a flavouring agent in Sri Lankan cuisine. Also known as rampe, has earned a reputation on TV cooking programmes and is being used in savoury and sweet dishes. Pandan leaves are available at Asian supermarkets, in the freezer section.

Panko breadcrumbs are coarsely ground, airy flakes used as a coating in Japanese cuisine. These crumbs produce a light, crunchy crust and tend to remain crisper for a longer period than ordinary breadcrumbs.

Pomegranate molasses is a thick syrup produced from pomegranate juice and a key ingredient used in Middle Eastern, Mediterranean and fusion cooking. It is a versatile souring agent that can be incorporated into marinades, dressings and dips.

White poppy seeds are traditionally used in Indian cuisine as a thickening agent and to flavour dishes. These tiny seeds are commonly used in the preparation of garam masala powder and other spice blends.

Ras el hanout is a highly aromatic spice blend from North Africa that has similar pungent properties to Indian garam masala. Used as a flavouring in many savoury dishes and marinades, it can be purchased from most major supermarkets.

Rose water has a delicate, sweet aroma and is often used in Indian, Sri Lankan and Middle Eastern cuisine to flavour cakes, desserts, sweets, jellies and milkshakes. It is also widely used in wedding rituals and religious ceremonies in India and Sri Lanka. Pure rose water can be found in the international aisle of most supermarkets.

Tamarind is one of the most widely used souring agents in Sri Lankan and Indian cuisine. It has a sweet and tangy taste and is available in many forms, such as compressed blocks, pastes and concentrates. Usually available in the international aisles of the major supermarkets or from Sri Lankan, Indian and Asian grocery stores.

Toor dal is a type of legume that looks very similar to split yellow peas. It is considered to be protein and fibre rich and is used in making sambar, a traditional lentil soup, and other lentil dishes.

Urad dal is also known as black gram and it is one of the most widely used, highly valued pulses in Sri Lankan and Indian culinary preparations. It is the main ingredient in dosa and is also highly regarded by vegetarians as the most nutritious legume.

IN THIS CHAPTER, I SHARE WITH YOU THE SPECIAL SPICE POWDERS THAT I LIKE TO USE IN MY COOKING. FRESHLY GROUND SPICES ARE WELL WORTH THE TIME AND EFFORT. PREPARE THESE AHEAD OF TIME SO THEY ARE ON HAND WHEN YOU NEED THEM.

SPICE BLENDS

JAFFNA STYLE CURRY POWDER

For generations, my family prepared curry powder at home. A unique blend of carefully selected ingredients are measured to precise proportions, dry roasted and then milled into a powder. Jaffna curry powder is chilli based and it adds the most incredible flavour to curries.

- 1 cup coriander seeds
- 20–25 dried, long red chillies, cut into two pieces
- 1–2 Tbsp black peppercorns
- 2 Tbsp cumin seeds
- 2 tsp fennel seeds
- 1 tsp fenugreek seeds
- 2 sprigs of curry leaves

1. Place all the ingredients except the cumin and fenugreek seeds in a heavy-based pan. Dry roast on medium heat for 15–20 minutes. Add the cumin and fenugreek seeds and heat through for 2–3 minutes. Continuously stir to prevent the spices from burning! The spices will be aromatic and change to a golden brown colour. Remove from the heat and set aside to cool in the pan.

2. Grind into a fine powder and store it in an airtight container, in a cool, dark place. It will keep fresh for up to 6 months.

DARK-ROASTED AROMATIC SPICE POWDER

My mother's dark-roasted aromatic spice powder has the potential to transform a meat curry into an extraordinary dish. If you are looking for a totally authentic Sri Lankan flavour in your meat curry, then you will need this spice powder.

- 2 cups coriander seeds
- 20–25 dried chillies
- 1 tsp fenugreek seeds
- 2 Tbsp black peppercorns
- ½ cup cumin seeds
- ½ cup fennel seeds
- 15–20 cloves
- 15–20 cardamom pods
- 12cm cinnamon stick
- 2 sprigs of curry leaves

1. Place all the ingredients in a heavy bottom pan and gently roast for 15–20 minutes. Continuously stir to avoid burning the spices. The spices will be aromatic and turn to a golden brown colour and the dried chillies will darken around the edges. Remove from the heat and cool in the pan. Grind into a fine powder and store in an airtight jar. Store in a cool, dark place and it will keep for up to a month.

2. It is also a good idea to mill only the quantity that you need and store the roasted, whole ingredients in a jar for later use.

EASY RASAM POWDER

Even though ready-made rasam powders are readily available at major grocery stores, I make my own blend fresh every time. I always stick to my favourite, easy-to-remember ratio.

½ cup coriander seeds
¼ cup cumin seeds
⅛ cup black peppercorns

1 Place all the ingredients in a dry grinder and mill into a coarse powder. Store in an airtight jar.

MIXED ALLSPICE POWDER

This sweet-smelling spice powder is an essential, powerful ingredient used in Sri Lankan Love Cake and rich fruit cake recipes. Discover this easy-to-make, aromatic blend and bring new depths to your baking!

6 cardamon pods
3cm Sri Lankan cinnamon stick
4 cloves

1. Grind the cardamom pods, cinnamon stick and cloves into a fine powder. Store the ground spice in an airtight container, in a cool, dark place. It can be kept for up to a week.

INDIAN MASALA POWDER

This is my grandmother's version of garam masala that she used in some of her recipes to achieve authentic Indian flavours. This is not too pungent and works brilliantly to flavour the dishes.

2 Tbsp cumin seeds
2 Tbsp coriander seeds
½ Tbsp black pepper
8–10 cloves
½ Tbsp mustard seeds
12–15 cardamom pods
2 Tbsp fenugreek seeds
2 Tbsp urad dal
2 Tbsp chana dal
2 Tbsp fennel seeds
6cm cinnamon stick
1 star anise
¼ of a nutmeg
1 dried mace
1 Tbsp poppy seeds

1. Dry roast the ingredients individually until golden and aromatic. Using a dry grinder, process the roasted ingredients into a fine powder and store in an airtight jar. Keep it in a cool, dark place for up to a month.

ROASTED FENNEL POWDER

Roasted fennel powder is an absolute must-have in my pantry and it is an essential spice in my lamb, chicken and some vegetable curry recipes. Once the curry is made, simply sprinkle this aromatic spice over for flavour enhancement.

⅛ cup cumin seeds
½ cup fennel seeds
1 sprig of curry leaves

1 Place all the ingredients in a heavy-based frying pan and lightly roast for 8–12 minutes. Continue to stir until golden brown in colour and highly aromatic. Remove from the heat and set aside to cool in the pan. Grind into a fine powder and store in an airtight container, in a cool, dark place. It will keep fresh for up to a month.

SAMBAR POWDER

Sambar spice is an essential condiment. It is used in sambar, a lentil-based vegetable broth popular in South India. Here is our family recipe, which has been tried and tested for generations.

100g dried red chillies
100g coriander seeds
50g chana dal
50g toor dal
¼ cup black peppercorns
a chickpea-sized piece of asafoetida*
*If you are unable to find solid asafoetida, use one Tbsp of the powdered variety.

1 Lightly dry roast the asafoetida in a heavy-based pan. Then individually roast each spice until nicely golden and fragrant. Roast the peppercorns until aromatic. Combine and set aside to cool. Grind into a powder and store it in an airtight container, in a cool, dark place. It will keep for up to 6 months.

STAPLES/ BASICS

SUPER PUTTU

My genius brother-in-law came up with this idea for a low GI, protein rich puttu. Traditionally, puttu is made with rice flour and cooked in a purpose-made, cylindrical steamer. My version of this super healthy, delicious puttu is ideal for weeknight dinners and a great substitute for cooked rice.

For roasted super-grain flour mix
½ cup quinoa flour
½ cup amaranth flour
½ cup sorghum flour
½ cup millet flour
½ cup brown spelt flour

For the puttu
½ cup couscous
½ cup roasted red rice flour
½ cup roasted super-grain flour mix
1¾–2 cups of boiling water
1 cup fresh coconut, grated
salt to taste
extra brown spelt for dusting

SERVES 4–5
PREP 30 MINS
COOKING 45 MINS

To make roasted super-grain flour mix
1. Place all ingredients in a microwave-proof bowl. Microwave on high for 2–3 minutes and mix well. Continue this roasting process a couple more times. This flour mix should be roasted evenly and have a fresh baking aroma. Stir well.

To make the puttu
2. Place the couscous, roasted rice flour, salt and roasted super-grain flour mix in a large metal bowl.

3. Add boiling water gradually and stir continuously with a fork or a wooden spoon. The mixture should form into a lumpy nugget-like texture.

4. Cool slightly and break it down with your hands or pulse in a food processor until the lumps disintegrate into peppercorn-sized nuggets. If you find the pieces to be too sticky, dust with extra spelt flour and toss lightly with your fingertips.

5. Set up the steamer according to the manufacturer's instructions. Layer the steamer compartment loosely with a cup of prepared puttu mix and then spread a Tbsp of grated coconut over this.

6. Repeat this process until the steamer is almost filled. It is important not to pack it too tightly.

7. Put on the lid and position the steamer over the base pot containing boiling water. Cook for 10–15 minutes or until steam starts to escape rapidly through the lid.

8. Remove the steamer and transfer the cooked puttu onto a serving platter.

DOSA

Dosa are an everyday food served for breakfast in India. They are protein rich and taste amazing with sambar, coconut chutney, and potato masala, which are the traditional vegetarian accompaniments. I like to serve them with Jaffna fish curry and coconut sambal.

1½ cups idli rice or short grain rice
1 cup urad dal (polished black gram)
¼ cup coarse semolina
salt to taste
oil spray or oil
water

SERVES 6–8
PREP 30 MINS
+ SOAKING
+ FERMENTING
COOKING 45 MINS

1 Wash the rice and urad dal separately and soak with plenty of water in separate bowls for 4–5 hours. Rinse a few times and drain.

2 Grind the rice in a food processor with a bit of water until you get a smooth, thick batter. Pour into a large mixing bowl. Repeat this process with the dal.

3 Add the ground dal to the rice paste. Add the salt, semolina and mix well to combine. This batter should have a mousse-like consistency. Cover and set aside in a warm place to ferment overnight. It should double in size.

4 Place a frying pan or dosa griddle over a medium-high heat.

5 Check the consistency of the fermented batter first. Gradually add water until it reaches a pancake batter consistency.

6 Into a small dish, put a couple of Tbsps of cooking oil. Dip a paper towel in the oil and wipe the griddle to coat the base evenly.

7 When the griddle is hot, ladle the batter in the middle and smooth it out with the back of a spoon into a thin layer. Cook for 1–2 minutes or until the edges begin to turn lightly golden, then flip over. Once both sides are lightly golden and crispy, transfer to a plate. Serve warm.

 When processing the dal batter, add the water gradually. It is difficult to define the precise water quantity! With trial and error, you will be able to master the art of making perfect dosa.

UPPUMA

Uppuma makes a delicious rich savoury accompaniment to many meat dishes. I particularly like serving it with a spicy masala chicken.

½ cup coarse semolina
¼ cup tomato, diced
½ cup onion, diced
1 red chilli
¼ tsp ginger
1 tsp chana dal
Salt to taste
1 sprig of curry leaves
1 Tbsp oil
½ tsp mustard
¼ tsp cumin
¾ cup water

SERVES 2-4
PREP 20 MINS
COOKING 30 MINS

1. Place the semolina in a shallow pan and dry roast for 4-5 minutes, or until it just begins to turn golden. Set aside.

2. Heat the oil in a saucepan and fry the mustard and cumin seeds. As they begin to sputter, add the chana dal and fry for 1 minute.

3. Add the ginger, onions, chilli and curry leaves, and sauté until the onion softens and caramelises around the edges.

4. Add the chopped tomatoes and salt, and cook for 3-4 minutes until soft. Stir in the roasted semolina and mix well to coat with the tomato mixture. Remove and set aside.

5. In the same pan, pour the water and bring to a boil. Gradually incorporate the semolina mixture and stir continuously until the water is absorbed and the mixture is fluffy. It is important not to mix the semolina too quickly as this will result in a lumpy uppuma.

APPAM/HOPPERS

Appam is a popular Sri Lankan breakfast dish shaped like a round bowl with wafer-thin edges. The combination of spongy sourdough centre and the crispy edges are utterly delicious. This recipe is quick to prepare and makes perfect hoppers every time.

3 cups coarse rice flour
4 Tbsp self-raising flour
3 Tbsp caster sugar
2½ tsp instant dry yeast
2 cups warm water
salt to taste
1 cup coconut milk
½ cup sparkling water
oil

MAKES 18–20
PREP 30 MINS
+ FERMENTING
COOKING 45 MINS

1 For this recipe you will need a hopper wok. You can buy these from Sri Lankan grocery stores. If a hopper wok is unavailable, use a small regular wok.

2 Place the rice flour, self-raising flour, 2 tsp of sugar and yeast in a large bowl.

3 Add the 2 cups of warm water and mix well to create a smooth batter. The consistency should be similar to cake batter. Cover and set aside in a warm place for 3–4 hours.

4 Gradually mix the coconut milk, sparkling water and remaining sugar with the fermented rice batter and mix well to combine. Set aside for 30–45 minutes.

5 Grease the hopper wok. If you are using a non-stick wok, do not grease it as this will make it too slippery for the batter to cook on the edges.

7 Heat the hopper wok with the lid on. Ladle about ½ a cup of batter into the wok. Lift and swirl the batter to coat the sides.

8 Place the wok back on the stove, cover, and cook for 2–4 minutes or until the sides are crispy and golden.

9 Carefully release the hopper with a palette knife. Transfer to a plate and serve with coconut sambal and curries of your choice.

To make the egg hoppers spoon the batter into the heated wok, lift and swirl around to coat the sides. Place the wok back on the stove, break an egg in the centre, cover and cook for about 2–3 minutes. Sprinkle with salt and black pepper.

DOSA, PAGE 46.

MINI ROTI

These mini roti are super easy to make and go with just about anything you can imagine.

1 cup wholemeal flour
½ cup self-raising flour
½ tsp red chilli, finely chopped
½ tsp green chilli, chopped
½ tsp cumin seeds
1 Tbsp olive oil
¾ cup warm water
salt to taste

MAKES 20
PREP 45 MINS
COOKING 30 MINS

1. Place all the ingredients except the water in a large bowl.

2. Make a well in the middle and gradually add the water, mixing and kneading for 15 minutes until you have a smooth dough.

3. Divide the dough into ten lime-sized balls, cover with a damp kitchen towel and set aside for 30 minutes or more.

4. Take each ball of dough, divide in half and roll it with your palm into a small ball.

5. Flatten each ball into a mini pancake shape and cook each side for 45 seconds in a heated frying pan.

SWEET PASTRY/SHORTCRUST

300g plain flour
60g ground almonds
150g icing sugar
170g chilled butter, cubed
2 egg yolks
1 tsp almond essence
1–1½ Tbsp iced water

SERVES 6–8
PREP 30 MINS
COOKING 30 MINS

1. Preheat the oven to 180°C.

2. Place the flour, almonds and icing sugar in a food processor and mix to combine. Add butter and pulse together until the mixture resembles breadcrumbs.

3. Mix the eggs, almond extract and water and pulse until it just comes together. It is hard to specify exact water quantity so add the water gradually, one spoon at a time until the mixture forms the dough.

4. Turn out onto a lightly floured bench and knead to form a disc. Cover with plastic wrap and refrigerate for half an hour. Don't overwork the pastry!

5. Using softened butter, grease the tart tins of your choice. This recipe makes enough for 2 tins of 25cm diameter or 8 mini tart tins. I recommend using tins with a removable base.

6. Roll out the pastry thinly (about ½cm thickness), cut to into circles and line the greased tins. Chill the pastry-lined tins in the refrigerator for 20 minutes.

7. Place a piece of baking paper over the chilled pastry, fill with baking weights and blind bake for 8–10 minutes.

8. Remove the tins from the oven and take the baking weights out. Cook for a further 8–10 minutes or until the pastry is lightly golden around the edges. Due to the sugar in the pastry, it will brown easily. Keep a close watch!

V

CHICKEN STOCK

2 chicken frames cut into small pieces
1½ cups red onion, sliced
1 cup carrot, sliced
1 cup leek, sliced
5cm piece of ginger
15 peppercorns
salt to taste
6 cups water

MAKES 3 CUPS
PREP 10 MINS
COOKING 45 MINS

1 In a saucepan, boil all the ingredients for 40–45 minutes until the liquid reduces to half. Strain and set aside.

SHORT EATS/ SAVOURY BITES

AVO + PRAWN CROSTINI, PAGE 72.

IN SRI LANKA, 'SHORT EATS' REFERS TO A VARIETY OF SAVOURY SNACKS. SIMILAR TO TAPAS, THESE MORSELS ARE IDEAL FOR SERVING AS FINGER FOOD AT COCKTAIL OR DINNER PARTIES. THIS CHAPTER SHOWCASES SOME OF THE SHORT EAT RECIPES THAT ARE CLOSE TO MY HEART.

CRUNCH 'N' SPICE MIX

A simple, healthy snack made with nuts and seeds, this is great for kids' lunchboxes, or with drinks of an evening!

¾ cup roasted chana dal
¾ cup pumpkin seeds
¾ cup sunflower seeds
¼ cup chia seeds
½ cup rice flakes
100g cashew nuts
¼ cup soy sauce
1 tsp honey or natural sweetener
½ Tbsp pomegranate molasses
20 curry leaves, cut into thin ribbons
1–2 tsp curry powder
½ tsp cumin seeds
a pinch of asafoetida powder
2 cloves of garlic, minced
salt to taste
oil spray

SERVES 10–15
PREP 15 MINS
COOKING 30 MINS

1. Heat the oven to 180°C. Place the soy sauce, curry powder, salt, garlic, curry leaves, asafoetida, cumin seeds, honey/sweetener and pomegranate molasses in a bowl, and whisk until combined.

2. Transfer the seeds, nuts, rice flakes and chana dal into the bowl with the spice mixture and mix well to coat.

3. Bake for 15–20 minutes, stirring the mixture at regular intervals.

4. Remove from the heat and set aside to cool. The crunch 'n' spice can be stored in an airtight container for up to two weeks.

A sweet, nutty dish matches well with a crisp light lager. Low-carb beers like DB Export 33 and Pure Blonde have little to no residual sugars and balance very well with this snack.

MY HOMEMADE SPRING ROLLS

When my children were young, they returned home from school expecting something yummy to yummy to eat, and my homemade spring rolls are the snack they loved the most. A crispy pastry encases a savoury filling made with shredded cabbage, chicken and a touch of garlic. Simply delicious served with my homemade dipping sauce.

For the filling
- ½ cabbage
- ½ cup kale, finely shredded
- 1 cup poached chicken meat, shredded
- 1 onion, diced
- ½ cup spring onions, finely sliced
- 1 Tbsp salt reduced soy sauce
- 1 Tbsp rice wine vinegar
- 1 clove of garlic, minced
- salt to taste
- freshly ground black pepper to taste
- 2 tsp peanut oil

For the spring roll pastry
- 125g plain flour
- 1 tsp baking powder
- salt to taste
- 2 Tbsp oil or melted butter
- 4–5 Tbsp water
- vegetable oil for deep frying

For the dipping sauce
- 6 dried red chillies, coarsely ground
- 3 Tbsp sugar
- ¼ cup white vinegar
- ¼ cup rice wine vinegar

To make the filling

1. Wash and finely shred the cabbage. In a pan heat two tsps of peanut oil and fry the minced garlic for 25–30 seconds, until golden. Add the onion and salt, and fry for 1–2 minutes until soft and aromatic.

2. Stir in the cabbage and cook for 2–3 minutes then add the chicken, kale and spring onions. Cook for 6–7 minutes.

3. Add the soy sauce and rice wine vinegar. Mix well to combine. Remove from the heat and set aside to cool.

To make the pastry

4. Mix the flour, baking powder and salt in a bowl. Gradually work in the melted butter (or oil) and water to form a stiff dough. Knead on a lightly floured surface for 5–10 minutes until smooth. Divide into small lime-sized balls, cover with a damp cloth and set aside for 2 hours.

To make the rolls

5. Roll out each piece of dough into a circle. Very lightly dry out each side in a frying pan. It takes less than 30 seconds to dry out both sides. I use an electric roti maker that flattens the dough and makes a great roti-like sheet for this purpose. Do not overcook the pastry as doing so will make it impossible to roll.

6. Mix half a cup plain flour with a little water into a paste. Use this to dampen four areas of the circle, then place 1 tsp of filling in the centre of each and tightly roll. Tuck in the two opposite ends before you roll up the dough circle, making sure that the edges hold together firmly.

¼ cup dark soy sauce
2 cloves of garlic
3cm piece of ginger
1 pink shallot
1 tsp peanut oil

MAKES 12–15
PREP 60 MINS
COOKING 45 MINS

7 Heat sufficient vegetable oil in a deep frying pan. Drop a few spring rolls at a time into the hot oil and fry until they are crispy and golden. Drain and place on a tray lined with 4–5 layers of paper towels to absorb the excess oil. Serve hot with the dipping sauce.

To make the dipping sauce
8 Place the pink shallot, garlic, ginger and ground chilli in a food processor and blend to a coarse paste.

9 Heat the peanut oil in a saucepan, add in the chilli mixture and cook for 1 minute, stirring until it is aromatic. Add the sugar, soy sauce, white and rice wine vinegars and bring to a boil. Gently simmer for 8–10 minutes, until the sauce is reduced by half and thickens. Remove from the heat and transfer to a sterilised jam jar.

FISH CUTLETS

Sri Lankan fish cutlets are an all-time favourite that will impress even the most seasoned foodies. A spicy fish mixture coated with breadcrumbs and deep fried, these delicious cutlets are served warm with dipping sauces.

400g fish fillets
2 potatoes, boiled, peeled and flaked
salt to taste
1 tsp chilli powder
1 tsp turmeric powder
1 white onion, finely chopped
1 tsp fresh ginger, grated
2 green chillies, finely chopped
10 curry leaves, shredded
2 tsp curry powder (Jaffna style)*
2 Tbsp fresh lime juice
2 cups bread crumbs
freshly ground black pepper to taste
oil for deep frying
1 cup all-purpose flour
*Refer to Spice Blends chapter.

MAKES 18–20
PREP 30 MINS
COOKING 45 MINS

1. Boil the fish with half a cup of water, salt, turmeric and chilli powder for 15 minutes. Set aside to cool. Carefully remove any bones, flake with a fork and transfer to a bowl with the potatoes. Alternatively, fresh fish can be substituted with canned fish.

2. In a frying pan, heat 1 tsp of oil and sauté the chopped onion, ginger, chillies and curry leaves until the mixture is lightly browned and fragrant. Add curry powder, cook for 1–2 minutes and remove from the heat.

3. Transfer the onion mixture into the bowl with the fish and potatoes. Season with salt, pepper and lime juice and stir well to combine.

4. In a separate bowl, mix the flour, a pinch of salt and ground black pepper. Add enough water to create a smooth, thin batter and set aside (about 1 cup).

5. Divide the mixture and shape into golf ball-sized portions. Dip these balls in the prepared batter and roll in bread crumbs.

6. Heat sufficient oil for deep frying in a pan over medium-high heat. Cook the crumbed fish balls in batches until they are golden brown. Serve hot with tomato or chilli sauce.

CRAB CAKES W/ MANGO CHILLI AIOLI

I created this crab cakes recipe following an inspiring trip to Fisherman's Wharf in San Francisco. They are spicy and tangy and make for excellent finger food at parties.

For the crab cakes

- 2–3 large crabs (about 250g crab meat)
- 4 pink shallots, chopped
- 3 Tbsp fresh coriander leaves, chopped
- 1 Tbsp chives, chopped
- 1 red chilli, finely chopped
- ¼ tsp turmeric powder
- 1 tsp fresh ginger, grated
- ½ tsp cumin seeds
- 1 medium potato boiled and flaked (about 150g)
- 1 tsp lime juice
- salt to taste
- 1 egg, beaten
- 2 cups panko crumbs
- oil

For the mango chilli aioli

- ¾ cup mayonnaise
- 1–2 red chillies
- 2 garlic cloves
- ½ cup semi-ripe mango pieces

MAKES 10–12
PREP 30 MINS
COOKING 30 MINS

To make the aioli

1. Process the mango pieces, chilli, garlic and mayonnaise in a food processor. Refrigerate until required.

To make the crab cakes

2. Wash the crabs thoroughly. Cook them in salted, boiling water for 5–8 minutes. Drain the water and set aside to cool slightly.

3. Remove the outer shell and the greenish brown gut and discard. Carefully separate the crab meat and transfer to a large bowl and set aside.

4. Heat 1 tsp of oil in a frying pan and sauté the onion, ginger and chillies until the onion turns translucent. Remove from the heat and transfer into the bowl with crab meat.

5. Combine the crab meat, flaked potato, turmeric powder, onions mixture, lime juice, chives and coriander leaves. Make into golf ball-sized balls. Flatten each ball between your palms to make a disc.

6. Dip the crab cakes in the beaten egg and roll in panko crumbs. Heat oil in a frying pan and shallow fry the crab cakes on low to medium heat for 2–3 minutes on each side, until they are golden.

7. Serve warm with mango chilli aioli and garnish with coriander leaves.

This recipe can easily be made gluten-free by substituting the panko for gluten-free breadcrumbs.

SAMBAL + GOAT CHEESE TARTLETS

Seeni sambal is a spicy Sri Lankan relish made with onion, tamarind, chilli, spices and small dried anchovies. It pairs beautifully with creamy rich goat feta. These tartlets are great as a canapé if you are looking to serve something unexpected and full of flavour.

2 large onions, sliced
12cm piece pandan leaf
½ cup small dried anchovies
2 tsp red chilli flakes
6cm cinnamon stick
6 cardamoms
8–10 cloves
1 sprig of curry leaves
a golf ball-sized tamarind
1 cup water
1–2 Tbsp oil
4 Tbsp sugar
salt to taste
3 sheets savoury shortcrust pastry
200g goat feta, cut into small chunks

SERVES 4–6
PREP 30 MINS
COOKING 30 MINS

To make the pastry cases

1. Preheat the oven to 180–200°C. Grease mini tartlet tins. Cut the pastry and line each tartlet tin. Chill in the refrigerator for 20 minutes.

2. Blind bake with baking weights for 8–10 minutes. Remove the baking weights and return to the oven for a further 8–10 minutes or until the pastry is lightly golden around the edges. Set aside to cool.

To make the seeni sambal filling

3. Wash the anchovies in warm water and drain. Using a mortar and pestle or spice grinder, grind the cinnamon, cardamom and cloves into a powder and set aside. Soak the tamarind in a bowl of water for a few minutes. Extract the pulp and discard the membranes and seeds.

4. Heat the oil in a pan, and sauté the onion, pandan leaves, curry leaves and salt until translucent and lightly browned.

5. Add the extracted tamarind pulp, anchovies, ground spices, sugar and chilli flakes, and let simmer for 15–20 minutes until the sauce thickens and becomes glossy. Set aside to cool.

6. Fill the tartlet shells with a spoonful of seeni sambal and top with chunks of feta. Bake at 180°C for 10–12 minutes or until the feta starts to soften.

To add dimension to the sweetness and richness of these tartlets, match with a beer with a strong hop aroma like Sawmill IPA. Some APAs and IPAs have more of a malt aroma, which will add sweetness to the overall flavour profile rather than achieve a balance.

CRAB CAKES WITH MANGO CHILLI AIOLI, PAGE 68.

SAMBAL + GOAT CHEESE TARTLETS, PAGE 69.

AVO + PRAWN CROSTINI

Fried prawns on toast was one of my dad's favourite party nibbles. His love of this dish inspired me to create this delicious canapé. Avocado offers a delightful contrast and balances the hot, spicy flavours, while the mango relish adds a sour fruitiness.

1 loaf of ciabatta, cut into slices
10 large prawns, peeled and deveined
4 tsp olive oil
1 tsp chilli flakes
1 tsp dill, finely chopped
1 tsp fennel seeds
¼ of a star anise
2 garlic cloves, finely chopped
salt and pepper to taste
2 avocados
1 tsp lemon juice

For the relish
1 medium sized, half-ripened mango, diced
1 red chilli, finely chopped
50ml white vinegar
2 Tbsp of caster sugar
30ml water
1 garlic clove, crushed
1 tsp white mustard powder
3–4 basil leaves
1 Tbsp coriander leaves
salt and pepper to taste

MAKES 10
PREP 45 MINS
COOKING 30 MINS

To make the mango relish
1. Place the salt, vinegar, sugar and water in a saucepan and heat until the sugar melts. Add the diced mango, chilli, mustard powder and basil leaves, and bring to a quick boil. Cook for 1–2 minutes until the liquid evaporates.

2. Add the crushed garlic and remove from the heat. Cover with cling wrap and set aside. Mix in the coriander leaves before serving.

To make the avo mash
3. Remove the skin of the avocado and scoop out the flesh into a bowl. Mix with lemon juice, salt and black pepper, and crush roughly with a fork.

To make the prawns
4. Place the prawns, oil, salt, chilli flakes, garlic and dill in a bowl. Coarsely grind the fennel seeds and star anise. Mix into the prawns. Cover and set aside to let the flavours infuse.

5. Sear the prawns in a hot frying pan for 2–3 minutes each side. Remove from the heat.

To serve
6. Fry the ciabatta for 2 minutes each side. Spread with avocado mash and assemble the prawns and relish on top.

Pair this dish with a Prosecco or an off-dry Riesling. The trick here is to have both sugar and acidity. These elements will balance the spiciness of the prawns and relish as well as the richness of the avocado.

FISH BUNS, PAGE 88.

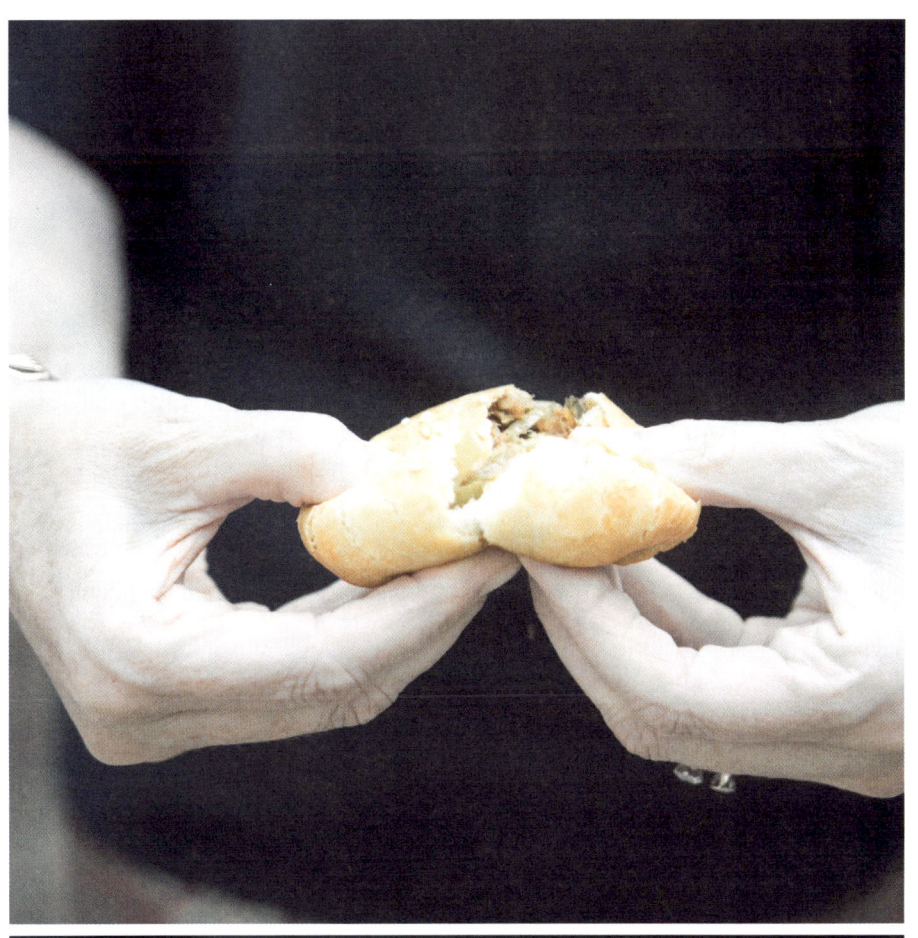
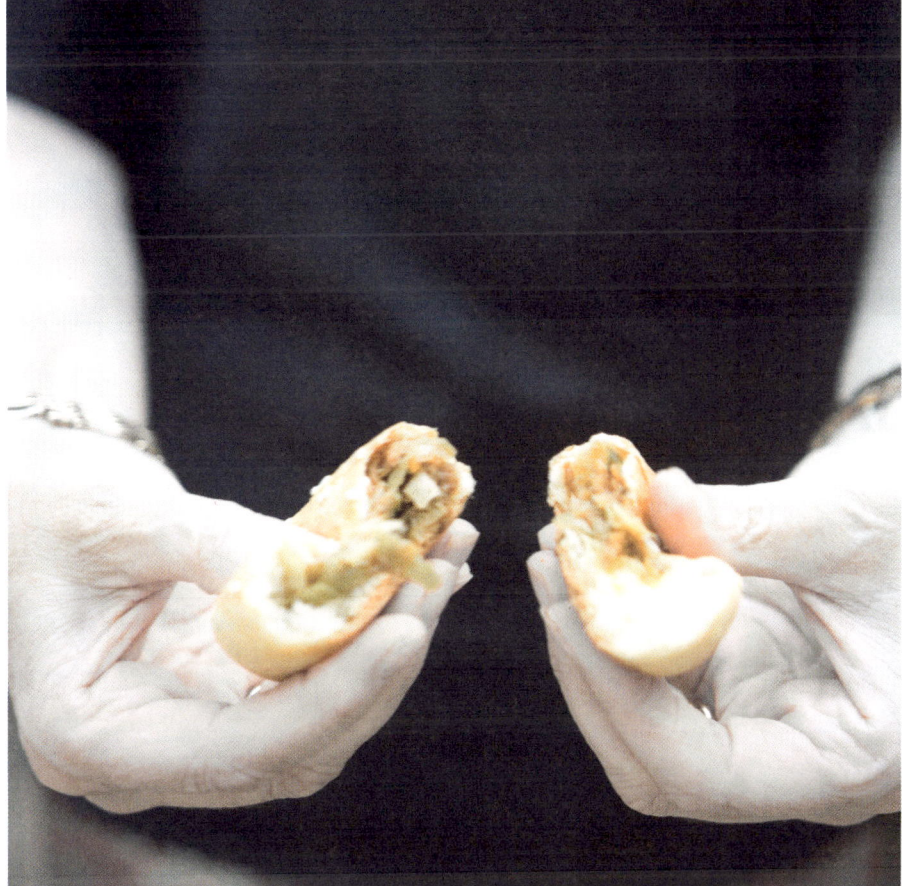

MINI PASTIES W/ OTAGO VENISON

These mini pasties are somewhere between a Cornish pasty and an empanada by way of Sri Lanka and Otago. This is a unique, easy recipe for a lunch or snack that's always a crowd pleaser.

500g venison mince
salt and pepper to taste
1 tsp dark-roasted aromatic spice powder*
1cm piece of ginger, finely chopped
1 clove garlic, finely chopped
1 tsp curry powder (Jaffna style)*
1 tsp oil or oil spray
1 small potato, peeled and diced into small cubes
1 cup red onion, finely diced
1 green chilli, finely chopped
6 curry leaves, rolled and sliced finely
¼ tsp roasted fennel powder*
3 tsp fresh lime juice
750g savoury shortcrust pastry sheets
1 egg yolk, beaten with 2–3 Tbsp milk, for glazing
*Refer to Spice Blends chapter.

To make the spiced venison filling

1 Place the venison mince in a bowl with salt, pepper, curry powder, dark-roasted spice powder, ginger and garlic.

2 Heat the oil in a pan and sauté onion, chilli and curry leaves until the onion is translucent and the mixture is fragrant.

3 Stir the venison mix and diced potatoes into the onion mixture, breaking down the mince with a spatula. Reduce the heat and simmer for 10–15 minutes or until meat is thoroughly cooked and the liquid has evaporated.

4 Sprinkle with roasted fennel powder, add lime juice and stir well. Set aside to cool.

To make the pasties

5 Preheat oven to 180°C. Cut the pastry sheets into circles approximately 10cm across.

6 Dampen the edges and place the venison filling in the middle. Enclose the filling by pinching the edges of the pastry together. Arrange the pasties on a lined baking tray. Using a pastry brush, glaze evenly with egg yolk mixture.

7 Bake for 25–30 minutes or until golden. Serve warm with sriracha or tomato sauce.

MAKES 20–30
PREP 60 MINS
COOKING 45 MINS

A good match for these is a beer that has both fruity notes and high carbonation to cut through the richness of the pastry. English-style ales like Coopers Pale Ale and Little Creatures Pale Ale are good examples of this.

MASALA VADAI

Masala vadai is a traditional South Indian snack that is also a popular street food in Sri Lanka. These little treats are great for vegans and are perfect with some tangy chutney on the side.

1 cup chana dal (split chickpeas)
1 medium red onion, finely chopped
1 green chilli, finely chopped
1 tsp ginger, finely grated
1 dried red chilli
½ tsp fennel seeds
½ tsp cumin seeds
6 black peppercorns
2 Tbsp coriander leaves, chopped
10 curry leaves, rolled and sliced finely
salt to taste
oil for deep frying

MAKES 20–25
PREP 60 MINS
COOKING 45 MINS

1. Soak the chana dal for one hour and drain well. Spread it on paper towels to remove the excess moisture.

2. Grind the chana dal coarsely in a food processor and transfer to a mixing bowl.

3. Coarsely grind the dried chilli, fennel, cumin, pepper and add to the chana mixture. Add the rest of the ingredients, except the oil, and mix well. The mixture should be slightly moist but not too soggy.

4. Take small handfuls of the mixture and make into balls. Gently flatten the balls between your palms to make little discs.

5. Heat the oil in a deep frying pan. Drop in a few discs at a time and fry until golden. Remove and drain on absorbent paper. Serve warm with coriander chutney.

CATTERY & KENNELS

Cherries
← Pick Your Own

SCALLOPS W/ OTAGO CHERRIES

Plump and juicy Central Otago cherries are abundant in the summer season and this recipe is is proof that cherries are not just for desserts!

500g scallops

For the herb butter
30g butter
1 tsp garlic, minced
1 tsp ginger, minced
1 green chilli
salt to taste
¾ cup flat leaf parsley, roughly chopped
¾ cup coriander leaves, roughly chopped
zest and juice of 1 lime

For the cherry sauce
1 cup cherries, diced
2 Tbsp balsamic vinegar
2 tsp white vinegar
2 Tbsp sugar
salt to taste
1 tsp garlic, minced
1 tsp ginger, minced

SERVES 4–6
PREP 30 MINS
COOKING 30 MINS

To make the herb butter
1. Place the garlic, ginger, salt, chilli, parsley and coriander leaves in a mortar and pestle or food processor and grind to a paste.

2. Transfer the ground ingredients to a bowl and mix with the butter, zest and lime juice. Refrigerate until required.

To make the cherry sauce
3. Boil all the ingredients listed for 8–12 minutes, or until the sauce thickens and coats the back of a spoon. Remove from the heat and set aside to cool.

To cook the scallops
4. Preheat the oven to 200°C. Line a baking tray with baking paper and arrange the scallops, leaving space between them.

5. Spoon a dollop of herb butter on top of each scallop and place the tray under a hot grill for 4–6 minutes.

6. Remove from the oven and serve with the cherry sauce.

Scallops are subtle in flavour, so you don't want a heavy accompaniment. Try a light, lemony pilsner like the Urbanaut Pilsner. A crisp, clean apple cider like Honesty Box Apple Cider is also good as it provides just enough sweetness to balance the chilli without being saccharine.

VADAI

Vadai is an indispensable item on most Sri Lankan Tamil's special event menus. This doughnut-shaped crispy snack is best eaten fresh from the pan while it is hot and crunchy.

For plain vadai

1½ cup urad dal
½ cup water
1 medium red onion, finely chopped
2 green chillies, finely chopped
1 tsp ginger, finely grated
15 curry leaves, rolled and sliced
1 pinch of asafoetida
salt to taste
oil for deep frying

For yoghurt vadai

½ cup Greek yogurt
2 Tbsp water
¼ tsp mustard seeds
4–5 curry leaves
¼ tsp chana dal
1 tsp oil
salt to taste

MAKES 15–20
PREP 30 MINS + SOAKING
COOKING 45 MINS

1. Soak the urad dal for 4 hours or overnight, drain well and place in a food processor. Add the water gradually and process until the mixture is slightly coarse, but thick and fluffy. It is better to add less water to get these crispy.

2. Transfer the batter to a mixing bowl and add the remaining ingredients.

3. Heat the oil in a deep frying pan. Take a small handful of the vadai mixture, place it in the palm of your hand, flatten slightly and make a hole in the centre with your index finger. Wet your hands each time before handling the dough.

4. Deep fry in batches until golden. Drain the fried vadai on paper towels.

Yoghurt vadai variation

5. Mix the yoghurt and water in a bowl.

6. In a frying pan, heat the oil and fry the mustard seeds. As they begin to sputter, add chana dal and curry leaves. Fry for a couple of minutes, then remove from the heat.

7. Reserve a small portion of this fried mustard, chana and curry leaves mix for garnishing and pour the rest over the yogurt.

8. Mix in chopped coriander leaves and salt. Dip the vadai into the seasoned yoghurt mixture. Garnish and serve hot.

FISH BUNS

Fish buns are one of the most popular snacks in Sri Lanka. A tasty fish filling encased in a soft dough, these buns are very moreish.

For the filling

370g cooked fish, flaked (e.g. tuna)
1 medium leek
1 medium carrot
1½ tsp oil
3 shallots, sliced
2 green chillies, finely chopped
8 curry leaves, rolled and sliced thinly
2 tsp curry powder (Jaffna style)*
1 clove of garlic, finely chopped
1 potato, boiled, peeled and flaked
1 tomato, diced
salt and pepper
1 Tbsp tomato sauce

For the buns

2 tsp yeast
1½ tsp sugar
1 cup warm water
500g plain flour
50g butter
1½ tsp salt
1 egg, lightly beaten
1 extra egg mixed with 1 Tbsp milk for glaze
sesame seeds for sprinkling (optional)
*Refer to Spice Blends chapter

To make the filling

1. Wash the leek and cut into small pieces. Peel and grate the carrot.

2. Heat the oil in a pan, sauté the shallots, chilli and curry leaves until the shallots are translucent. Stir in the curry powder and cook for 1–2 minutes.

3. Add the flaked fish, garlic, carrot, leek and potato and cook for 10–12 minutes. Add the diced tomato and cook until the mixture is relatively dry.

4. Add the tomato sauce and cook for a further 2 minutes. Set aside to cool.

To make the buns

5. Preheat the oven to 180°C. Mix yeast, sugar and water in a bowl. Cover and leave in a warm place until the mixture becomes frothy.

6. Put the flour and butter in a bowl and knead by hand or mix with a stand mixer using a dough hook at a slow speed for 2–3 minutes. Gradually pour in the yeast and beaten egg. Knead for 10–12 minutes until the dough is smooth and elastic.

7. Cover with a damp cloth and set aside for 1 hour, or until the dough doubles in size.

8. Punch down the dough. Roll the dough into golf ball-sized balls. Arrange on a tray lined with baking paper, leaving a gap of at least 15cm between each ball of dough. Set aside in a warm place to rise.

9. Flatten each ball of dough with your palm, place the fish filling in the middle and fold the edges over to cover the filling completely. Mould into a bun shape.

MAKES 16–18
PREP 60 MINS
COOKING 45 MINS

10. Place filled buns on the lined baking tray and set aside for 35 minutes to rise further.

11. Evenly glaze the buns using a pastry brush. Bake in the preheated oven for 25–30 minutes or until golden. Serve warm with tomato sauce or relish

Any leftover fish mixture makes a great toastie filling or is a tasty addition to a simple pasta sauce for a quick lunch.

GRILLED WHOLE PRAWNS + SALSA

I find prawns are so much more enjoyable when served with their shells on and eaten by hand. You might need to provide finger bowls and plenty of napkins!

8–10 prawns
freshly ground pepper to taste
salt to taste
4 cloves of garlic, minced
2 tsp hot chilli flakes
2 Tbsp coconut oil
1–2 Tbsp lime juice

For the salsa
1 medium avocado
¼ cup tomatoes, diced
1 red chilli, finely chopped
1 spring onion, finely chopped
¼ cup coriander leaves, chopped
juice of ½ a lime
salt and pepper to taste

SERVES 4–5
PREP 45 MINS
COOKING 30 MINS

To prepare the prawns

1. Leave the whole shell on, remove the heads, gently pull out the intestinal tract and discard. Rinse quickly and lay on a paper towel to absorb excess moisture.

2. Place the prawns in a bowl and season with salt and pepper. Add garlic, chilli flakes, lime juice and one Tbsp of the coconut oil. Mix well to combine. Cover with cling wrap and refrigerate for 1–2 hours to marinate.

To make the salsa

3. Cut the avocado in half and gently twist to remove the seed. Make cuts in the flesh in a criss-cross pattern. Scoop out the avocado pieces into a clean bowl.

3. Add the rest of the ingredients and mix lightly to combine. Refrigerate until needed.

To cook the prawns

4. Heat the remaining coconut oil in a wide frying pan. Cook the prawns over a medium-high heat for 3 minutes each side, or until cooked to your liking.

5. Serve straight away with salsa on the side.

MINI ROTI W/ CHICKEN HEARTS

Devilled chicken hearts encased in a warm roti is a beautiful appetiser that requires only a little bit of preparation. These tasty little treats can add a unique twist to your banquet menu.

For the devilled chicken hearts

450g chicken hearts
salt to taste
½ tsp turmeric powder
1 tsp curry powder (Jaffna style)*
a generous grinding of black pepper
½ tsp dark roasted spice powder*
2 tsp oil
½ tsp cumin seeds
2 cups onions, chopped
1-2 green chillies, sliced
½ tsp minced garlic
1 sprig of curry leaves
10cm piece pandan leaf
¼ cup coconut milk
¼ cup water
juice of ½ a lime
*Refer to Spice Blends chapter

MAKES 20
PREP 45 MINS
COOKING 30 MINS

For the mini roti

1 Refer to Staples chapter, page 52. Keep warm until required.

For the devilled chicken hearts

2 Prepare the chicken hearts by removing the visible fat and arteries. Cut in half lengthwise, rub with salt, turmeric, curry powder, ground pepper, and dark-roasted spice powder. Set aside.

3 Heat the oil in a frying pan and fry the cumin seeds for 10 seconds. Add the onions, chillies, garlic, curry leaves and pandan leaf. Sauté for 5-6 minutes until the mixture is soft and golden.

4 Add the chicken hearts and stir fry over high heat for 1 minute then reduce the heat and mix in the water and coconut milk. Simmer for 8-10 minutes or until almost dry.

5 Remove from heat, squeeze in the lime juice and mix well. Serve in warm mini roti.

QUAIL WITH EGGPLANT AND COUSCOUS, PAGE 106.

MEAT

While based in Dunedin, I developed a special appreciation of New Zealand's world class meat – grass-fed lamb, wild venison and free range poultry.

I hope you will love these simple, tasty dishes full of complex flavours.

MOROCCAN SPICED ROAST CHICKEN

Moroccan cuisine uses subtle blends of spices that are also commonly used in Sri Lankan cuisine. This flavoursome chicken roast is an excellent centrepiece for a family get-together or a hearty midweek dinner.

1½ kg fresh, whole chicken
4-5 whole peppercorns
4 cloves garlic
3cm piece ginger
¼ of a preserved lemon
1 Tbsp tomato paste
1 Tbsp mango chutney
2-3 almonds
2 Tbsp ras el hanout
1-2 Tbsp olive oil
juice of 1 orange
salt to taste
1 tsp chilli powder
6 baby potatoes

For the yoghurt dressing
1 cup Greek yoghurt
5-6 mint leaves, chopped
½ cup coriander leaves
1 green chilli, finely chopped
1 pink shallot, chopped
salt to taste
1 tsp sugar

SERVES 4-6
PREP 30 MINS
+ MARINATING
COOKING 120 MINS

To make the coriander yoghurt dressing
1. Mix all the ingredients in a bowl and set aside in the fridge for at least 30 minutes for the flavours to infuse.

To make the spice paste
2. In a food processor, grind the peppercorns, garlic, ginger, preserved lemon, tomato paste, chutney and almonds into a coarse paste.

3. Combine the ground paste with ras el hanout, oil, orange juice, salt and chilli powder in a bowl.

To prepare the chicken
4. Place the chicken in a large dish, pour the spice mixture over and rub well with your fingertips. Cover and set aside in the refrigerator for 6-10 hours or overnight.

5. Preheat the oven to 180-200°C. Place the chicken on a sheet of foil, tie the legs and wings with the kitchen string. Wrap the foil around the bird. Wash the potatoes, wipe dry, and rub with olive oil and salt. Lay the chicken and potatoes on a roasting tray.

6. Roast for 1-1½ hours or until juices run clear. Roasting time depends on the individual oven so check that the bird is not overcooked at this point. Unwrap the foil and bake for a further 15-20 minutes, or until nicely browned.

7. Remove from the oven, cover the chicken with a sheet of foil and rest for at least 10 minutes. Serve with yoghurt and your favourite salad.

Grenache and Zinfandel are commonly soft fruity wines that love a bit of spice. A soft Merlot-based Rosé, for example a Bordeaux Rosé, would also work well.

SIZZLING PEPPERED LAMB

These juicy, succulent pieces of lamb are such a treat when served sizzling. This is one of my favourite weeknight meals that requires only a little bit of preparation.

500g lean lamb, cut into 4cm x 1cm pieces
4 Tbsp caramelised onion salad dressing
4 tsp chermoula
salt to taste
a generous grinding of black pepper
2 Tbsp rice bran oil

For the orzo salad
¾ cup orzo pasta
¼ tsp freshly grated garlic
salt to taste
2 Tbsp lemon juice
2 Tbsp orange juice
½ Tbsp lemon zest
½ Tbsp orange zest
pepper to taste, freshly ground
1 Tbsp olive oil
½ cup red pepper, diced
½ stick celery, diced
1 spring onion, finely sliced
¼ cup raisins
¾ cup flat leaf parsley, finely chopped
¼ cup slivered almonds, lightly toasted

SERVES 4
PREP 30 MINS
COOKING 30 MINS

To marinate the lamb

1. Combine the salad dressing with chermoula, salt, and pepper. Place the lamb pieces in a bowl and pour the marinade in and mix well. Leave aside to marinate for 15–20 minutes.

To make the orzo salad

2. Cook the orzo according to the packet instructions, drain, and transfer to a bowl.

3. Whisk together the garlic, salt, juices, zests, ground pepper and olive oil. Add the prepared vegetables, raisins, nuts and parsley. Pour this mixture into the bowl of cooked orzo, and toss well.

To cook the lamb

4. Heat the oil in a non-stick frying pan over a high heat. Quickly sear the lamb pieces in batches for 1–2 minutes on each side.

5. Cover the cooked meat in aluminium foil and rest. Serve with the tangy orzo salad on the side.

Store-bought caramelised onion dressing is one of my favourite marinades but most salad dressings will work fine. Leftover lamb can be used in sandwich or a warm flatbread wrap.

ZIMBABWE CHICKEN

This chicken recipe had its beginnings on a family train trip when we lived in Zimbabwe. A fellow passenger opened their packed lunch and soon, pleasant mellow aromas filled the whole carriage. My children demanded that I create something similar and they named the dish 'Zimbabwe Chicken'. It has been a family favourite ever since.

500g skinless chicken thighs and drumsticks
¼ cup white vinegar
salt to taste
1 tsp coarse chilli powder
a generous grinding of black pepper
¼ cup water
2 tsp vegetable oil
1 large onion, sliced
a sprig of curry leaves
½ cup bell peppers, diced
2 green chillies, sliced

SERVES 4
PREP 30 MINS
COOKING 45 MINS

1. In a saucepan, place chicken, vinegar, salt, chilli powder, ground pepper and water. Cover with a lid and simmer on the stove for 10–12 minutes.

2. Remove chicken pieces from the pan and transfer to a bowl.

3. Bring the broth to a rapid boil and cook for 5 minutes to reduce. Set aside.

4. Heat the oil in a different pan and sauté the onions for 5 minutes until golden.

5. Add the chicken pieces, curry leaves, bell peppers and green chillies to the onion mixture and continue to stir fry for 4–6 minutes, or until the chicken pieces are nicely browned.

6. Add the reduced chicken broth to the chicken mixture and boil for 3–4 minutes. Remove from the heat and serve with rice or roti.

ZIMBABWE CHICKEN, PAGE 101.

LAMB RACK, PAGE 118.

THAI PORK CUTLETS W/ PINEAPPLE SALSA

My son-in-law introduced me to Nam Jim, a delicious Thai dipping sauce, which inspired me to design this recipe. Succulent pork pairs deliciously with the zing of vibrant pineapple salsa.

4 pork cutlets (about 150g each)
oil for brushing

For the Thai marinade
1 red chilli
1 green chilli
1 small bunch of fresh coriander
2 cloves garlic
1 small pink shallot
2 Tbsp fish sauce
2 Tbsp brown sugar
juice of 1 lime

For the salsa
½ cup fresh pineapple, finely diced
¼ cup cucumber, diced
¼ cup red pepper, diced
¼ cup green pepper, diced
¼ cup red onion, finely diced
salt to taste
pepper to taste, freshly ground
1 Tbsp lime juice

For the garnish
3 Tbsp chopped coriander leaves
2 tsp sesame seeds, toasted
micro cress

SERVES 4
PREP 30 MINS
+ MARINATING
COOKING 30 MINS

To make the marinade
1. Place all the ingredients in a blender and blitz until combined. Transfer to a bowl reserving 4–6 Tbsps for glazing.

2. Place the pork cutlets in the bowl with the prepared marinade and massage well on both sides. Set aside in the refrigerator for 4–5 hours.

To make the salsa
3. Place all the ingredients in a bowl and toss well to combine. Cover with cling wrap and refrigerate until required.

To cook the pork
4. Heat a grill pan. Brush the marinated pork cutlets with oil and cook over a high heat for 4 minutes. Turn over and cook for 2 minutes, reduce the heat to medium and continue to cook for 3–4 minutes, or until done.

5. Transfer the pork onto a plate and loosely wrap with foil and set aside to rest for 5 minutes.

To serve
6. Pile some salsa on a plate and sprinkle with chopped coriander leaves. Place a pork cutlet in the middle and lightly brush with the reserved marinade. Sprinkle sesame seeds and micro cress around the plate before serving.

QUAIL W/ EGGPLANT + COUSCOUS + TOMATO RELISH

A stunning combination of exotic spices and herbs brings out the best in the delicate quail meat. This delightful recipe delivers a touch of the master class!

4 quails (about 600g)
¼ of one star anise
½ tsp nigella seeds
¼ tsp cumin seeds
¼ tsp fennel seeds
¼ tsp black peppercorns
3cm piece of ginger
3 cloves garlic
1–2 fresh red chillies
1–1½ Tbsp mango chutney
juice of ½ a lime
1 Tbsp rice bran oil
1 Tbsp coriander leaves, chopped
1 Tbsp chopped parsley

For the tomato relish
200g mixed coloured cherry tomatoes
½ cup various coloured bell peppers, chopped
1 Tbsp olive oil
½ tsp nigella seeds
1 clove garlic, chopped
salt to taste
5–6 Tbsp white vinegar
1 tsp sugar or natural sweetener

For the couscous
1 cup couscous
salt to taste
2 Tbsp olive oil
1 clove of garlic, minced
1–2 tsp red chilli, finely sliced

To make the spice rub

1 Place the dry spices in mortar and pestle (or food processor) and pound into a powder. Then add the ginger, garlic and chillies, and grind until well crushed and incorporated.

2 Place the quails in a large dish. Add the mango chutney, salt, lime juice and freshly ground spice paste. Use your fingers to massage and coat the meat with the marinade. Transfer to a bowl, cover with cling film and set aside in the fridge for a minimum of 1 hour — longer for more robust flavours.

To make the tomato relish

3 Preheat the oven to 180°C. Line a baking tray with baking paper. Spread the tomatoes and bell peppers and mix with the olive oil, nigella seeds, garlic and salt to coat. Roast for 15–20 minutes, or until the skin is blistered.

4 Remove from the oven and peel off the skin from the bell peppers, dice into small cubes and transfer to a bowl. Transfer the roasted tomatoes including the skin, pan juices and residues into the same bowl with the peppers. Check the seasoning, add the sugar and mix well. Set aside until required.

For the couscous

5 Cook the couscous with salt according to the packet instructions. Fluff up the grains with a fork, cover and leave for 3–4 minutes.

6 Heat the olive oil in a non-stick pan and gently fry the garlic until golden. Add the chillies and fry for 15–20 seconds. Lastly, incorporate the nuts, currants and parsley and cook for 2–3 minutes, until the mixture is fragrant. Add the cooked couscous to this mixture and stir well to combine. Set aside until required.

- 1–2 tsp green chilli, finely sliced
- 2 Tbsp slivered almonds
- 2 Tbsp currants
- 2 Tbsp parsley, finely chopped
- freshly ground black pepper to taste

For the grilled eggplant
- 1 clove of garlic, grated
- 1 large eggplant (about 450g–500g)
- 3–4 Tbsp olive oil and extra oil spray for the pan
- salt to taste

SERVES 4
PREP 30 MINS + MARINATING
COOKING 45 MINS

To make the eggplant

7 Cut the top and tail off the eggplant, cut into 1cm thick slices and wash well. Drain and pat dry with paper towels. Rub with garlic, salt and oil.

8 Place a large frying pan over a medium heat and coat generously with oil. Grill the eggplant slices in batches for 2–3 minutes on each side, until soft and coloured. Set aside on a plate and keep warm.

To cook the quail

9 Preheat the oven to 200°C. Heat a large, ovenproof frying pan over high heat and add the oil. Quickly sear quails, breast side down for 2–3 minutes. Turn the birds over and cook for a further 1–2 minutes.

10 Place the pan with the birds in the oven for 5–6 minutes or until the quails are cooked through. Cover with foil and set aside to rest for 5 minutes.

To plate

11 Spoon the flavoured couscous in the middle of a large plate. Arrange the grilled eggplants on the side. Place a cooked quail on the couscous, dollop on the tomato relish along with the pan juices, and serve.

Overall the dish is low in fat and very perfumed so it's important to choose a wine that's not too intense. Quail is quite delicate as well and gamey so a savoury wine is preferred. A tomato relish like the one here requires a wine with acidity. Try a lighter style of Pinot Noir or a dry Northern Italian Red (e.g. Barbera, Sangiovese)

NOTHING EXCITES ME MORE
THAN EXPERIMENTING
WITH INGREDIENTS FROM
A DIVERSE RANGE OF
CULTURES. MY CURIOUSITY
ALWAYS LEADS TO
DELECTABLE AND EXCITING
COMBINATIONS.

THE SIMPLEST WAY TO ADD VARIETY TO WEEKNIGHT MEALS IS TO KEEP FRESH PRODUCE, ESSENTIAL HERBS AND SPICES ON HAND.

PAN-SEARED NZ LAMB W/ COUSCOUS + MINT SALSA

A stunning combination of lamb, lemony couscous and salsa makes a perfect meal at the end of a busy day! Basil and garlic infused olive oil, thyme, sea salt and black pepper are the simple enhancements to the lamb in this recipe. The minty salsa adds a bit of spicy amusement.

750g lamb leg steaks
a generous grinding of black pepper
4 tsp basil and garlic infused olive oil
salt to taste

For the couscous
1 cup couscous
salt to taste
juice and zest of ½ a lemon
3 Tbsp parsley, finely chopped
½ cup red pepper, diced
1 green chilli, finely sliced
1 clove of garlic, minced
2 Tbsp olive oil
1 Tbsp golden sultanas

For salsa
1 cup mint leaves
1 cup baby cavolo nero (Tuscan kale)
¼ cup sliced almonds
1 cup coriander leaves
2-3 cloves of garlic
2 green chillies
1 spring onion
salt to taste
juice of 1 lemon

For the couscous
1. Cook the couscous with salt according to the packet instructions. Fluff it with a fork and mix in the lemon juice and zest until combined. Cover and leave for 3-4 minutes.

2. Heat the olive oil in a non-stick pan and gently fry the garlic until golden. Add the chillies and diced pepper and fry for 25-30 seconds. Incorporate the sultanas and parsley and cook for 2-3 minutes, until the mixture is fragrant. Add the cooked couscous and stir well to combine. Cover and set aside.

To make the minty salsa
3. Place all the ingredients in a food processor and process it coarsely. Transfer into a small bowl, cover and refrigerate until ready to serve.

To cook the lamb
4. Trim excess fat from the lamb and remove the silver skin. Season with salt and pepper and rub with olive oil.

5. Heat a grill pan over high heat. Add the steaks and cook for 2-3 minutes on each side, or until meat is cooked to your liking. Cover loosely with foil and rest for 8-10 minutes.

6. Slice the lamb and serve over a bed of warm lemony couscous with salsa on the side.

SERVES 4
PREP 30 MINS
COOKING 30 MINS

Remember that cooking time depends on the thickness of the steak. It is best to serve the New Zealand lamb pink inside to preserve its succulent flavour.

LAMB LEG ROAST W/ HARISSA + ROASTED GARLIC

This recipe showcases my take on the classic New Zealand Sunday roast with a spicy twist. This roasting method is proven to produce juicy, tender meat.

1 leg of lamb (about 1kg)
15 cloves garlic, skin on
2 Tbsp harissa spice powder
2 Tbsp vegetable oil
salt to taste
1 Tbsp lemon
½ cup of water
4–5 small potatoes scrubbed
½ cup coriander leaves, chopped
handful of pistachios, chopped

For the harissa yogurt with pomegranate

1 cup natural yogurt
1 tsp sugar
1 tsp harissa spice powder plus ½ tsp extra for garnish
salt to taste
2 Tbsp pomegranate seeds
1–2 coriander sprigs

SERVES 4–6
PREP 30 MINS
+ MARINATING
COOKING 90 MINS

To cook the lamb

1. Preheat oven to 180°C. Place the garlic cloves on a lined baking tray and rub well with 1 Tbsp of oil. Roast in the preheated oven for 20–25 minutes until lightly coloured and soft. Remove the garlic from the tray and let cool.

2. Place the lamb in a roasting pan and make small, even incisions all over. Rub with salt and set aside.

3. Peel and place the roasted garlic in a bowl and mash it with a fork. Mix this garlic pulp with the harissa, lemon juice and the remaining olive oil. Rub this spice paste evenly over the lamb leg and place it in the roasting tray.

4. Rub the potatoes with a bit of oil and scatter around the lamb in the roasting tray. Cover with cling wrap and let it marinate for 2–3 hours.

5. Roast uncovered in a preheated oven at 240°C for 10 minutes. Then reduce the heat down to 180°C and cook for a further 30 minutes.

6. Pour the water around the edges, cover the pan with foil and cook for 15–20 minutes.

7. Switch off the oven. Check to make sure that the lamb is cooked to your liking. Keep covered with foil and leave it inside the oven for 10 minutes.

Lamb is fattier and gamier than most other meats and can handle a more tannic red wine, preferably savoury. However, it is important to take into account the spice of this dish. We recommend a Southern Rhone Red (GSM), or a Rioja Reserva. The key quality of these wines is the sweet oak element.

8 Transfer the cooked lamb and potatoes onto a warm serving tray. Scrape up the spice paste and juices from the pan and spoon over the lamb. Scatter with chopped coriander leaves and pistachios.

To make the harissa yoghurt

9 Mix all the ingredients together. Garnish with extra harissa, pomegranate seeds and coriander sprigs.

To serve

10 Garnish with extra coriander leaves and pistachios. Slice and serve the lamb with the pan juices, potatoes and harissa spiced yogurt.

SZECHUAN DUCK LEGS W/ COCONUT MILK RICE + PICKLED GINGER

This duck recipe has loads of contrasting textures and character. Rich duck meat is complemented with a warming sauce laced with ginger, red chillies, garlic and lemony Szechuan pepper. Mung dal adds flavour and bite to the milky, coconut rice.

For the duck

2 duck legs
1 red chilli, finely sliced
½ red onion, sliced
3 cloves garlic, finely chopped
2 tsp ginger, grated
salt to taste
1 orange
1½ Tbsp soy sauce
¼ cup water
2 Tbsp honey
1 tsp vegetable oil

For the garnish

1 red chilli, sliced
4–6 chives
1–2 courgettes, cut into ribbons

For the spice rub

1 tsp Szechuan pepper
¼ of a star anise
¼ of a whole mace
1 tsp coriander seeds
½ tsp cumin seeds
½ tsp fennel seeds
3cm cinnamon quill

For the coconut rice

1 cup basmati rice
1½ Tbsp mung dal (skinned and split), toasted
1¾ cups water
¼ cup thick coconut milk
a pinch of salt

SERVES 2
PREP 30 MINS
COOKING 60 MINS

1. Preheat the oven to 180°C.

2. Prepare the spice rub by lightly toasting all the spices for 2–3 minutes over a low heat until aromatic. Using a spice grinder, process into a coarse powder and set aside.

3. Place a deep frying pan over a medium heat. Rub the duck legs with salt and brown on each side for 3 minutes. Remove from the heat and transfer into an baking dish. Massage the ground spice all over the skin of the duck.

4. In a clean frying pan, heat the oil and sauté the ginger and garlic for 30 seconds. Add the chilli and onion, and cook for 2–3 minutes.

5. Mix the orange juice with the soy sauce and water. Stir and pour over the duck, then drizzle with honey. Cover with tin foil and bake in the preheated oven for 35–40 minutes. Remove the foil, cook for a further 10 minutes until the duck is cooked through and tender.

6. While the duck is in the oven, prepare the coconut rice. Rinse the rice and place in a saucepan with water and salt. Bring to a boil and cook over a medium heat for 10 minutes.

7. Stir in the toasted mung dal and coconut milk and cook for a further 5 minutes with the lid on. Remove from the heat and keep warm until required.

8. Serve the duck legs with coconut rice, garnished with chives, red chilli and courgette ribbons.

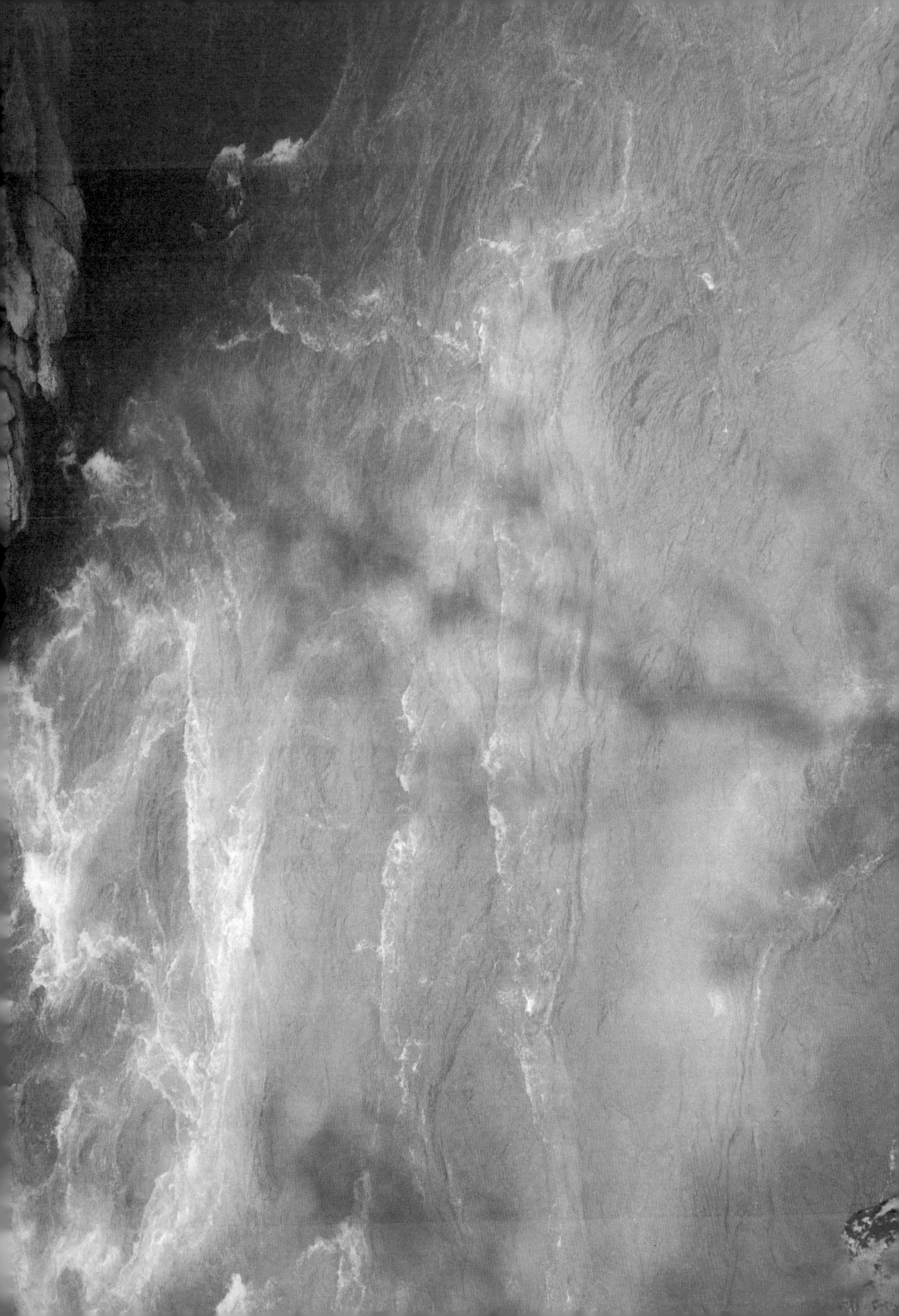

LAMB RACK W/ STUFFED MUSHROOMS + BABY CARROTS + CHERRY SAUCE

This tasty, hearty dish uses balanced layers of sweet, sour and umami to complement the wonderful qualities of New Zealand lamb.

For the lamb
400g lamb rack
½ tsp fennel seeds
½ tsp coriander seeds
½ tsp mustard seeds
salt to taste
freshly ground pepper
2 cloves of garlic, minced
2 tsp olive oil
2 sprigs of thyme
2 tsp rice bran oil

For the mushrooms
4–6 Portobello mushrooms
1 potato, boiled, peeled and flaked
1 rasher of bacon, finely chopped
1 green chilli, finely chopped
1 shallot, finely chopped
2 Tbsp chives, chopped
1–2 Tbsp cheese, grated
1 Tbsp mayonnaise
salt to taste
freshly ground pepper
zest of half a lemon
juice of half a lemon

For the herbed crumb
½ cup breadcrumbs
1 sprig of thyme
4 Tbsp parsley, chopped
zest of half a lemon
1 Tbsp butter

1. Grind the spices coarsely. Place the lamb rack on a platter and rub with salt and pepper. Combine the ground spices, garlic, olive oil, thyme and massage evenly over the lamb. Cover with cling wrap and set aside for 1–2 hours.

For the veges

2. Prepare the filling for the mushrooms by mixing the ingredients in a bowl. Make the herbed crumb by blending all the ingredients in a food processor.

3. Remove the stalks from the mushrooms. Divide the filling mixture equally and pile on the flat side of the mushrooms. Top with the herbed crumb and press firmly. Arrange on a lined baking tray and set aside.

4. Preheat oven to 180°C. Place the baby carrots in a bowl with oil, balsamic vinegar, garlic and salt and toss to combine. Spread on a baking tray, lined with baking paper and bake for 30–35 minutes, until cooked

5. Place the filled mushrooms in the hot oven and bake 10–12 minutes, or until the crumb topping turns golden. Keep warm until required.

To cook the lamb

6. Heat the oil in a heavy oven-safe frying pan. Sear the lamb on each side for 2 minutes, until browned. Finish off the lamb rack in the oven for about 10 minutes. It is best to serve this cut of lamb pink inside.

For the baby carrots
16–20 baby carrots, washed and trimmed
2 tsp olive oil
1 tsp balsamic vinegar
1 clove of garlic, minced
salt to taste

For the cherry sauce
1 shallot, finely chopped
10 cherries, stones removed
1 cup vegetable stock

SERVES 4
PREP 45 MINS
COOKING 60 MINS

7 Transfer the lamb to a shallow dish, cover with foil and set aside to rest for 5 minutes.

For the sauce
8 Discard any excess fat from the roasting tray and place on the stove. Cook the shallots and chopped cherries in the lamb juices for 2–3 minutes until soft.

9 Add the vegetable stock and boil until the sauce reduces to desired thickness.

To serve
10 Carve and serve the lamb with stuffed mushrooms, cherry sauce and baby carrots.

A stout like Kilkenny or Murphy's echoes the depth of the lamb's flavour. Stouts are often nitrogenated which has a 'mellowing' effect. Guiness also pairs nicely although it is a slightly more bitter stout.

GRILLED MASALA CHICKEN W/ UPPUMA + ONION RAITA

I designed this South Indian-inspired meal for a hearty midweek dinner. This recipe requires the meat to be marinated for a few hours, so start the preparations well ahead of time. Onion raita adds a pleasant tangy sweetness to this dish.

500g chicken maryland
1 tsp chilli powder
1 tsp garam masala powder*
2 Tbsp harissa powder
2 cloves of garlic, minced
salt to taste
½ cup natural yoghurt
¼ cup coriander leaves, chopped
¼ tsp fresh ginger, grated
1 Tbsp mango chutney
1 tsp butter
2 Tbsp lemon juice

For the onion raita
¾ cup natural yoghurt
½ cup red onions, sliced
1 green chilli, sliced
salt to taste
¼ tsp sugar

*Refer to Spice Blends chapter.

SERVES 2–4
PREP 30 MINS
+ MARINATING
COOKING 45 MINS

1. Place the chicken in a bowl and pierce the skin with a fork. Add the salt, chutney, masala, harissa, lemon juice, chilli powder, garlic, ginger, coriander leaves and yoghurt. Massage well with your hands. Cover the chicken with cling wrap and refrigerate for 4–5 hours.

2. Preheat the oven to 180°C. Line a baking tray with baking paper, lay out the chicken and dot with butter. Bake for 25–30 minutes, or until cooked. Cover with foil and let rest for 5–8 minutes.

To make the uppuma
3. Refer to Staples chapter, page 47.

To make the onion raita
7. Mix all the ingredients together in a bowl. Serve on the side of the grilled masala chicken and fluffy uppuma.

A drier, spicy, savoury Gewurztraminer or a Southern Rhone White blend are very aromatic with nice texture while retaining refreshing acidity. They make great food wines. A Vouvray would also work as it is fresh with a touch of sweetness. Be aware that the higher the alcohol level, the more the heat of the chilli will be accentuated.

CRISPY SKIN DUCK W/ FENNEL PUREE + TAMARIND SAUCE

A unique spice blend of fennel, peppercorns and star anise provides an incredible backdrop to the rich duck meat. This dish makes for an elegant entree or main.

4 duck breasts (about 150g each)
1 tsp garlic, minced
salt to taste
2 sprigs of thyme

For the spice rub
¼ of one star anise
¼ tsp fennel seeds
½ tsp black peppercorns
2-3 dried red chillies
2cm cinnamon stick

For the tamarind sauce
lime-sized piece of compresssed tamarind
1 cup water
5 dates, chopped
4 Tbsp jaggery or palm sugar
¾ tsp grated ginger
a pinch of salt

For the fennel purée
250g fennel bulb
2 garlic cloves
salt to taste
1 cup milk
2 Tbsp cream cheese

For the garnish
200g lotus root, thinly sliced
rice paper, broken into pieces
oil for deep frying
baby beetroot leaves
salt to taste

SERVES 4
PREP 30 MINS + MARINATING
COOKING 45 MINS

For the tamarind sauce
1 Soak the tamarind in water for a few minutes. Extract the tamarind pulp and discard the membranes and seeds. Place the tamarind and the remaining ingredients in a saucepan and cook over a low heat for 10-12 minutes. The sauce should be thick enough to coat the back of a spoon. Pass it through a fine sieve and set aside.

For the spice rub
2 Place all the ingredients in a frying pan and dry roast for 2-3 minutes. Remove from the heat and grind into a powder. Score the duck breast and season with salt. Sprinkle over 2 tsp of the ground spice, massage it well and set aside for 1-2 hours.

For the fennel purée
3 Rinse and slice the fennel bulb and place it in a saucepan. Add the milk, garlic cloves and salt, and boil for 15 minutes. Transfer to a blender, add the cream cheese and blitz until smooth. Set aside and keep warm until ready to serve.

To cook the duck
4 Preheat the oven to 180°C. Fry the duck breast skin side down with thyme sprigs in an ovenproof frying pan for 2-3 minutes. Turn the duck breast over and quickly fry the other side for 30-40 seconds. Place the frying pan inside the oven for a further 5 minutes.

5 Remove the pan from the oven, cover with foil and let rest in a warm place for 5 minutes. The duck skin should be golden brown and the flesh should still be pink and moist.

To serve
6 Deep fry the lotus root slices until golden. Fry the rice paper until it puffs up.

7 Slice the duck breast, drizzle with the tamarind sauce and serve with the fennel puree. Garnish with lotus root, rice paper puffs and beet leaves.

TAGINE-STYLE VENISON

Tender pieces of delicious venison, coated with exotic spices and combined with the sweetness of dried fruits, tangy pickled lemon and tomato, tastes utterly delightful. There is no better way of showcasing New Zealand's delicate venison!

1 kg venison, diced
salt to taste
½ tsp ginger, minced
½ tsp garlic, minced
1½ tsp Kashmiri chilli powder
1½ Tbsp harissa powder
2 Tbsp chermoula powder
2 Tbsp oil
1 large onion, sliced
½ a red capsicum, sliced
1 Tbsp tomato paste
prunes, seedless dates and dried apricots (3 each)
½ cup raisins
¼ pickled lemon, pips removed and finely chopped
1 Tbsp fresh lemon juice
1 ripe tomato, chopped
½ tsp turmeric powder
1–2 cups water
coriander leaves for garnish

SERVES 6–8
PREP 30 MINS
+ MARINATING
COOKING 90 MINS

1. Rub the meat with salt, garlic, ginger, chilli powder, harissa and chermoula spices. Set aside for 10–15 minutes.

2. Heat half the oil in a saucepan over medium heat and sauté the onion and capsicums until soft and fragrant. Remove cooked onion mixture and set aside.

3. In the same pan, heat the remaining oil and cook the marinated venison over a high heat until browned. Do it in batches if necessary. Transfer the venison and the onion mixture to a pot. A Sri Lankan clay pot works perfectly but any saucepan with a lid will work fine.

4. Add the tomato paste to the pot and cook on the stovetop for 1–2 minutes, stirring the mixture occasionally.

5. Stir in the dried fruits, pickled lemon, lemon juice, chopped tomato and water. Cover and cook over a low heat for 1–1½ hours or until the meat is tender and each piece is coated well with the spicy sauce. Stir the mixture periodically to make sure that the sauce doesn't burn on the bottom of the pot. Remove from the heat.

6. Garnish with chopped coriander and serve with pilaf, plain rice or couscous.

This dish has quite a bit of tang from the fruit, so you need a wine with enough acidity that it doesn't taste flat. It should also be delicate so as not to overpower the venison. Try a dry Rosé, which is serious and savoury. A light and savoury Martinborough Pinot Noir would also work. Avoid oaky Pinot Noirs here.

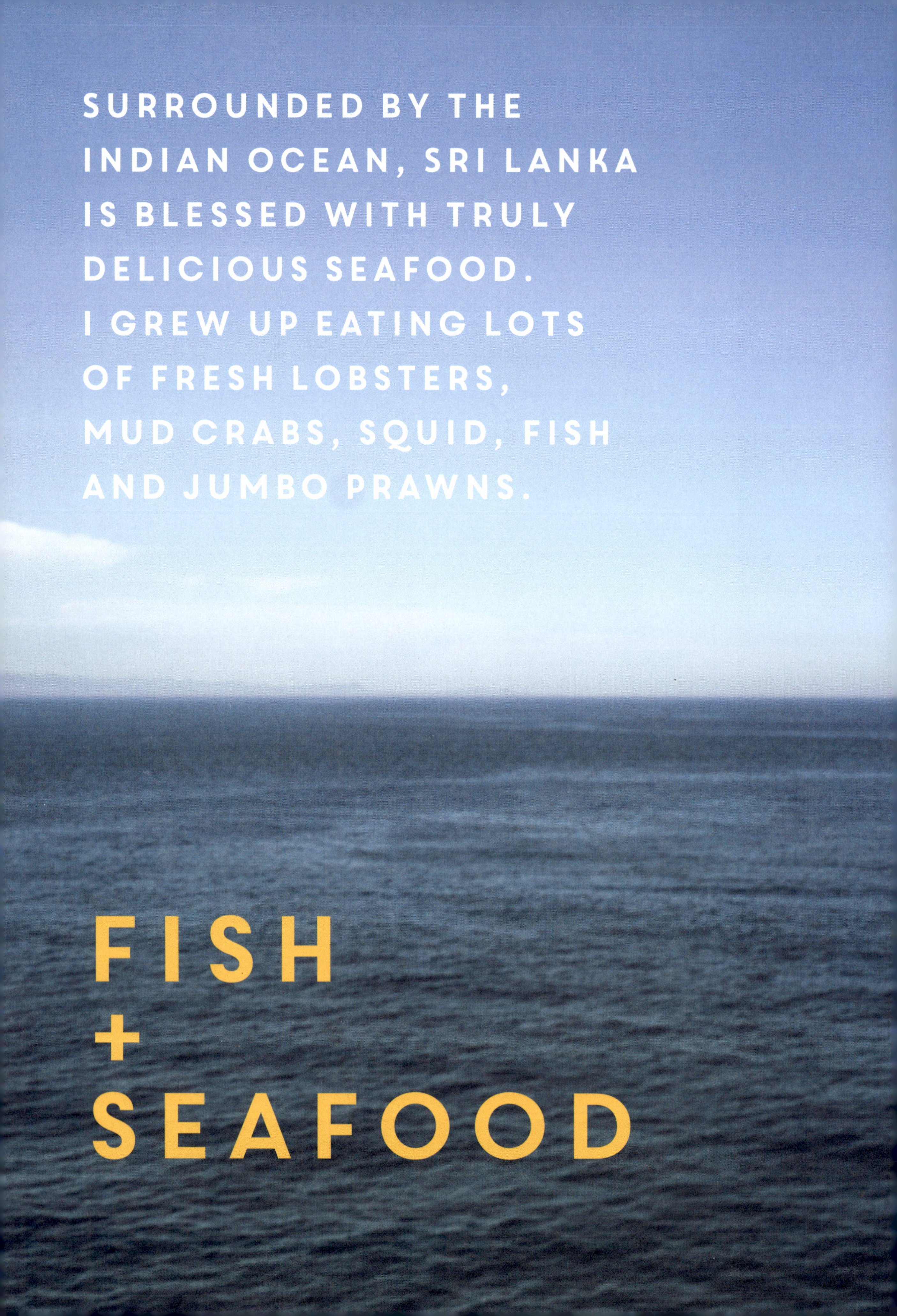

SURROUNDED BY THE
INDIAN OCEAN, SRI LANKA
IS BLESSED WITH TRULY
DELICIOUS SEAFOOD.
I GREW UP EATING LOTS
OF FRESH LOBSTERS,
MUD CRABS, SQUID, FISH
AND JUMBO PRAWNS.

FISH
+
SEAFOOD

THE RECIPES IN THIS SECTION TAKE INSPIRATION FROM MY CHILDHOOD MEMORIES AS WELL AS THE ABUNDANT AND VARIED SEAFOOD OF AUSTRALIA AND NEW ZEALAND.

HAPUKA W/ CAULIFLOWER PURÉE + CHERRY TOMATOES + PAKODA

A showstopper meal that is well worth the effort.

700–750g hapuka fillets, skin on
1–2 Tbsp oil
2 tsp oak smoked salt*
freshly ground black pepper

For the pakoda
1 cup chana dal
1 red onion, sliced
2 green chillies
½ tsp fennel seeds
20 cashew nuts
15 curry leaves
½ tsp cumin seeds
oil for deep frying
salt to taste

For the cauliflower purée
500g cauliflower, cut into florets
1½ cups water
2 garlic cloves, crushed
1cm piece of ginger, chopped
½ tsp cumin seeds
1 tsp oil
½ cup fresh milk
salt to taste
1 Tbsp mango chutney

For the roasted tomatoes
200g cherry tomatoes
2 cloves of garlic, finely chopped
3 tsp extra virgin olive oil
2 tsp oak smoked salt*

To make the pakoda
1. Soak the chana dal for 1 hour, drain and spread on two layers of paper towels.

2. Place the dal, onion, chillies, fennel, cashew nuts and cumin seeds in a food processor and grind into a coarse paste. Add the salt and mix well.

3. Heat the oil in a pan. Pinch a small amount of mixture with your fingertips, shape into small nuggets and drop into the hot oil. Fry until the nuggets turn a golden brown colour. Remove and drain on paper towels and set aside until required.

To make the roasted tomatoes
4. Preheat the oven to 200°C. Place the tomatoes in a bowl and sprinkle with oak smoked salt. Stir in the garlic and olive oil until the tomatoes are coated.

5. Line a baking tray with baking paper and spread the cherry tomatoes on it. Bake for 20 minutes. Remove and set aside.

To make the the cauliflower purée
6. Heat the oil in a saucepan over medium heat and fry the cumin seeds for 30 seconds. Add the garlic and ginger, and sauté for 4–5 minutes. Stir in the cauliflower florets and salt. Cook for a further 5 minutes, or until the cauliflower begins to soften.

7. Add the milk and simmer until the cauliflower is cooked and the liquid is reduced. Transfer to a food processor with the mango chutney and process to a smooth purée.

If oak smoked salt is unavailable, use ordinary salt.

SERVES 4
PREP 30 MINS
+ SOAKING
COOKING 45 MINS

To make the hapuka

6. Score the skin and rub the fish fillets with oak smoked salt, ground pepper and oil. Heat a frying pan, spray with oil and fry the fish on a high heat for 3 minutes, skin side down.

7. Turn over and fry the other side for 3 minutes, or until the fish is cooked through.

8. Serve the fish with a few pieces of pakoda, a scoop of purée and the roasted tomatoes. Garnish with pea sprouts and microgreens.

CRAYFISH W/ HERBS + CHILLI

This is my take on a classic Kiwi summer delicacy. The slight kick of the chilli and herbs adds another dimension to the crayfish's complex, delicate flavours. This is quick and easy on the barbeque for Christmas or whenever you feel like celebrating.

2 medium-sized crayfish (whole or use tails)
75g butter, softened
salt to taste
freshly ground pepper to taste
1 clove of garlic, minced
½ tsp fresh ginger, grated
½–1 red or green chilli, finely chopped (to taste)
¼ cup coriander leaves, chopped
juice and zest of 1 lime, plus extra lime wedges to serve
1 Tbsp chives, chopped
If you are using live crayfish, please kill humanely after freezing until they are unconscious.

1. On a chopping board, lay each crayfish on its back and cut in half lengthwise. Remove the yellowish parts and discard. Pat dry with paper towels and set aside.

2. In a bowl, mix the butter, salt, black pepper, garlic, ginger, chillies and coriander leaves with the lime zest and juice. Use the food processor if you are making larger quantities.

3. Spread the butter mixture over the fleshy side of crayfish.

4. Preheat the oven to 180°C. Line a baking tray with baking paper and place the crayfish shell side down. Bake for 15–18 minutes.

5. Alternatively, cook the crayfish on a hot barbeque for 4–5 minutes.

6. Serve garnished with chives and extra lime wedges.

SERVES 2–4
PREP 45 MINS
COOKING 20 MINS

It is important with your beer match not to overpower the sweetness of the crayfish. A light international lager like Tsing Tao works well. Alternatively, a light, lemony pilsner will balance the heat of the chilli.

PANKO CRUSTED FISH + SPICY MISO

I love the mellow, salty, savoury taste of miso. Thanks go to my daughter who introduced me to this low calorie ingredient with plenty of adaptability. This dish is a powerful display of Asian flavours.

700–750g snapper fillets (4 pieces), skin on
2 packets good quality instant miso soup
4 spring onions, white and green parts separated
5cm piece ginger, grated
1–2 red chillies, finely chopped
8 basil leaves, rolled and sliced very thinly
6 Tbsp peanut oil
4 medium courgettes, sliced
1 Tbsp butter
1 cup panko crumbs
3 cups chicken stock*
salt to taste
1–2 tsp sugar or natural sweetener
juice of 1 lime, plus extra wedges for serving
*Refer to chicken stock recipe on page 56

SERVES 4
PREP 30 MINS
COOKING 60 MINS

1. Preheat the oven to 200°C. Slice the green part of the spring onions into fine rings. Slice the white part into julienne strips for garnishing.

2. Place the grated ginger and sliced green spring onions in a heatproof bowl. In another heatproof bowl, combine the red chilli and finely sliced basil leaves.

3. Heat the peanut oil in a frying pan until smoking hot. Pour half of the heated oil into the ginger and spring onion mixture and the other half into the chilli mixture. Set aside until required.

4. In a separate pan, sauté the courgettes in the butter. Divide equally among four serving plates and keep warm.

5. Brush the fish pieces with oil and sprinkle with salt. Using the same pan, sear the fish skin side down for one minute. Turn and cook the other side for another minute. Brush the fish with the ginger and spring onion oil mixture, sprinkle with panko crumbs, and grill in the preheated oven for 6–8 minutes.

6. While the fish is in the oven, bring the chicken stock to a boil, then remove from the heat. Mix miso soup packet contents and sugar into the hot stock and whisk to combine.

To serve

7. Carefully ladle the hot miso broth onto the plate. Place the grilled fish and courgettes on top and garnish with julienned spring onions and lime wedges. Add lime juice to the chilli and basil oil and drizzle it around the fish.

I use 10g packets of Mitoku instant miso soup (white with tofu) in this recipe. If you are unable to find instant miso soup, replace it with the same measure of white miso paste.

STUFFED BAKED CRABS

This dish is a family favourite. I based it on a dish my eldest sister used to make. My son-in-law jokes that he decided to propose to my daughter the minute he tried my stuffed crabs!

- 6 large blue swimmer crabs (about 5 cups of crab meat)
- 1 tsp butter
- 2 green chillies, finely chopped
- 3 Tbsp pink shallots, finely chopped
- 2 tsp flat leaf parsley, chopped
- 1 cup potatoes, boiled and flaked
- 4 Tbsp chives, chopped
- 3 Tbsp mild cheese, grated
- 2 Tbsp mayonnaise
- freshly ground pepper
- 4 cups premium quality breadcrumbs
- 2 Tbsp extra butter for baking
- salt to taste

For the tartare sauce
- 6 Tbsp mayonnaise
- 2 gherkins, finely chopped
- 1 tsp capers, finely chopped
- 2 Tbsp flat leaf parsley, finely chopped
- 4 Tbsp chives, finely chopped
- 2 pink shallots, finely chopped
- juice of one lemon

SERVES 6
PREP 120 MINS
COOKING 30 MINS

To make the tartare sauce
1. Mix all the sauce ingredients in a small bowl, adding the lemon juice last. Stir well and refrigerate until required.

To make the crabs
2. Thoroughly rinse the crabs and cook them in salted, boiling water for 5–8 minutes. Drain the water and set aside to cool slightly. Carefully remove the outer shells, rinse and wipe them dry with paper towels. Keep the shells in the refrigerator until required.

3. Separate the crab flesh and transfer to a large bowl and set aside.

4. Heat the butter in a pan and sauté the shallots and chillies. When lightly golden, stir in the parsley and cook for 1–2 minutes. Remove from the heat.

5. In a large bowl, gently mix the crab meat, sautéed shallot mixture, flaked potatoes, chives, cheese, mayonnaise and ground pepper. Check the seasoning and add more salt if necessary.

6. Pack the reserved crab shells with the crab mixture. Sprinkle breadcrumbs on top and refrigerate for 1 hour. Dot with extra cold butter and bake in the oven preheated to 180°C for 15–20 minutes, or until the tops turn golden.

7. Serve warm with tartare sauce and leafy greens.

Acidity is key here, and there are lots of options. Try an Albarino (always a good choice for seafood) or a Gruner Vetliner. An elegant French Sauvignon Blanc (Sancerre) will also work well. These wines will bring out the herbal elements in the dish. Another great pairing would be a Champagne.

ITALIAN STUFFED SQUID W/ ORZO

An abundance of courgette and fresh squid during the summer season inspired me to make the most of these gorgeous ingredients. I designed this recipe with only a few items from my pantry. This squid dish makes a great starter and I think it is a perfect way to incorporate Italian flavours into your cooking.

For the stuffed squid

- 2–3 medium sized squids (about 250g each, gutted, cleaned, with tentacles and wings intact)
- 1 clove garlic, minced
- 1 pink shallot, finely sliced
- 1 red chilli, finely diced
- 2–3 small courgettes, finely diced
- 2–3 Tbsp parsley, finely chopped
- extra parsley for garnish
- 1 cup cooked orzo
- 2 Tbsp oil
- salt to taste

For the tomato sauce

- 450–500g cherry tomatoes
- 1 red pepper, diced
- 1 Tbsp olive oil
- 1 tsp nigella seeds
- 2 cloves garlic, minced
- salt to taste
- 1 red chilli, finely diced (optional)
- 8–10 basil leaves
- 2 cups chicken stock or water

SERVES 4
PREP 45 MINS
COOKING 60 MINS

To make the roasted tomato sauce

1. Preheat the oven to 200°C. Coat the tomatoes and peppers with olive oil, nigella seeds, garlic and salt. Line a roasting pan with baking paper and spread the tomatoes and peppers onto it. Roast them in the oven for 15–20 minutes, or until the skins are blistered. Remove from the oven and stir in the basil leaves. Set aside in the pan until required.

To make the stuffing

2. Dice the squid wings and tentacles into small pieces. Save a couple of full-length tentacles for plating. Set aside the main tube of the squid body for stuffing.

3. Heat 1 Tbsp of oil in a frying pan and gently fry the garlic with the shallots and chilli for 1–2 minutes, until fragrant.

4. Add the courgette pieces and stir fry over a medium heat for 3–4 minutes. Mix in the diced squid and parsley. Cook for 5–6 minutes.

5. Stir in the cooked orzo, salt and mix well to combine. Remove from the heat.

6. Fill the squid tubes with the orzo mixture and secure with a toothpick.

To make the squid

7. Heat the remaining oil in a frying pan. Brown the stuffed squid tubes and the remaining tentacles, 2 minutes on each side.

8. Transfer browned squid tubes to the pan with the roasted tomatoes, pour in the chicken stock, cover loosely with foil and bake for 20–25 minutes at 180°C. Add extra water if it gets too dry. Remove from the oven.

To serve

9. Discard the toothpicks and slice the squid into even-sized pieces. Spoon tomato sauce onto each serving plate and place the sliced squids in the middle. Arrange the tentacles decoratively, garnish with parsley.

FISH SOUP W/ COCONUT MILK + CORIANDER

This spicy soup was inspired by my favourite Sri Lankan rice porridge — pulli kanji. What I most like about this soup is the ease of preparation and the combination of incredible flavours.

800g mild white fish (e.g. groper or snapper)
75g prawns, peeled and deveined
½ tsp cumin seeds
½ tsp mustard seeds
5 pink shallots, chopped finely
2 cloves garlic, finely chopped
2 green or red chillies, finely chopped
2 sprigs of curry leaves
2 tomatoes, chopped
½ tsp turmeric powder
½ Tbsp curry powder (Jaffna style)*
¾ cup basmati rice, rinsed and drained
½ cup coconut milk
5–6 cups hot water
1 cup coriander, chopped
salt to taste
juice of 1 lemon
extra lemon wedges to serve
*Refer to Spice Blends chapter

1. Cut the fish into bite-sized pieces.

2. Heat the oil in a saucepan and fry the cumin and mustard seeds. As the seeds begin to sputter, add the chopped shallots, garlic, chilli and curry leaves. Sauté until the mixture turns slightly golden.

3. Add the chopped tomatoes, turmeric, curry powder and cook for 1–2 minutes.

4. Stir in the rice and mix well, making sure each grain is coated with the spicy sauce.

5. Pour in the coconut milk and water. Let simmer for 15–20 minutes until the rice is cooked.

6. Add the fish pieces and prawns to the broth and cook on a high heat for 6–8 minutes. Scatter chopped coriander leaves and remove from the heat.

7. Squeeze in the lemon juice and serve hot with extra lemon wedges and crusty bread on the side.

SERVES 6
PREP 30 MINS
COOKING 30 MINS

CHILLI + GARLIC CRUSTED SALMON W/ HARISSA YOGHURT

Superbly tender salmon is crusted with spicy and lemony panko crumbs. A creamy spiced yoghurt rounds off the dish.

500g salmon fillets, skin on
3–4 Tbsp panko crumbs
1 tsp lemon zest
1 tsp garlic, finely grated
1 tsp chilli flakes
olive oil for brushing
salt to taste

For harissa spiced yogurt
1 cup natural yogurt
2 tsp harissa spice blend
1 tsp sugar or natural sweetener
salt to taste

For the garnish
a few sprigs of coriander
1 tsp harissa spice blend

SERVES 2
PREP 30 MINS
COOKING 30 MINS

For the yoghurt
1 Mix all the ingredients in a bowl. Garnish, cover with cling wrap and refrigerate.

To cook the salmon
2 Preheat the oven grill to 200°C.

3 Brush the salmon generously with olive oil, sprinkle with salt and set aside.

4 Mix the panko crumbs, garlic, lemon zest and chilli. Cover and set aside.

5 Heat a large, non-stick or grill pan over a high heat and cook the salmon, skin side down for 3 minutes. Remove from the heat.

6 Turn the salmon skin side up. Scatter the panko crumb mix over the skin and place under the grill for 2–3 minutes, until the crust is lightly golden.

7 Serve with spiced yoghurt and leafy green salads of your choice.

 Use gluten-free breadcrumbs instead of panko for a gluten-free option. These are readily available from most supermarkets.

ALL-IN-ONE SPANISH FISH

I am fascinated by Spanish cuisine, so I created this delicious recipe for a simple weeknight meal. It is very easy to prepare and makes a wholesome dish.

400g sole or turbot fillets
2 potatoes, peeled and boiled
2 medium tomatoes, sliced
1 red chilli, finely chopped
4 cloves of garlic, minced
2 pink shallots, finely sliced
1 fennel bulb, thinly sliced
1 red pepper, thinly sliced
2 tsp Spanish paprika
1 tsp curry powder (Jaffna style)*
1 cup fresh parsley, chopped
zest of 1 lemon
juice of 1 orange
freshly ground black pepper
salt to taste
4 Tbsp extra virgin olive oil

For the green salad

120g baby rocket leaves
2 Tbsp extra virgin olive oil
juice of ½ a lemon
salt to taste
*Refer to Spice Blends chapter.

SERVES 2-3
PREP 30 MINS
COOKING 30 MINS

1. Preheat the oven to 185°C. Slice the potatoes into 1cm thick slices.

2. Grease a baking tray with olive oil. Arrange the potato slices on the baking tray and top with sliced fennel, shallots, red peppers, garlic, chilli and thyme sprigs. Drizzle with 1 Tbsp of olive oil and bake for 10-12 minutes.

3. Remove the potatoes from oven and layer the tomato slices on top. Sprinkle with 1 tsp of paprika, chopped parsley and bake for a further 6-7 minutes.

4. Remove the tray from the oven and trickle the orange juice over the potato mixture. Arrange the fish on top, sprinkle with salt, remaining paprika, ground pepper, curry powder, extra chopped parsley and lemon zest. Drizzle with remaining olive oil. Bake for 10-12 minutes, or until golden around the edges.

5. While the fish is in the oven, prepare the rocket salad by tossing all the ingredients together.

6. Serve the fish bake with lemon wedges and rocket salad.

STUFFED BAKED CRABS, PAGE 136

COD W/ ROMESCO SAUCE + WILTED GREENS

I created this meal with flaky cod, romesco sauce, roasted potato slices, fennel and colourful rainbow chard to celebrate the spirited flavours of Spanish cuisine.

400g cod fillets, cut into 4 pieces
1 medium potato
150g fennel bulb, sliced
1 tsp Spanish paprika
salt to taste
freshly ground black pepper
3 Tbsp extra virgin olive oil

For the wilted greens
150g rainbow chard, rinsed
1 clove of garlic, crushed
1 tsp olive oil
salt to taste

For the romesco sauce
250g tomatoes
10 almonds, toasted
3 cloves of garlic, skin on
3 long dried red chillies
2 Tbsp extra virgin olive oil
1 Tbsp red wine vinegar
¼ tsp sugar or natural sweetener
salt to taste

SERVES 2
PREP 30 MINS
COOKING 30 MINS

To make the romesco sauce

1. Soak the dried chillies in hot water for 30 minutes. Discard the water and pat the chillies dry with paper towels.

2. Preheat the oven to 185°C. Place the tomatoes on a baking tray and roast for 20 minutes until the skin is lightly coloured and blistered. Add the garlic cloves and roast for a further 6-7 minutes. Remove from the oven and set aside to cool. Turn the oven up to 200°C.

3. Peel the roasted tomatoes and garlic. Place in a food processor with the toasted almonds and chillies. Process until smooth, then add the olive oil, red wine vinegar, sugar and salt, and blitz until combined. Transfer the sauce to a bowl, cover, and set aside for a couple of hours for the flavours to develop.

To make the potatoes and fennel

4. Peel, rinse and slice the potato into ½ cm discs. Arrange on a lined baking tray with the sliced fennel. Drizzle with 2 Tbsps of olive oil and sprinkle with salt. Bake in the hot oven for 25 minutes or until the potato slices are nicely golden. Remove from the oven and set aside. Leave the oven on for the fish.

To make the wilted greens

5. Heat the oil in a saucepan over medium-high heat. Add the crushed garlic and fry for few seconds until aromatic. Then add the chard, cover and cook for 1-2 minutes until wilted. Add salt and remove from the heat.

To cook the fish

6 Pat the fish fillets dry with a paper towel and rub with oil, paprika and pepper. Heat a non-stick frying pan over high heat and cook the cod skin side down for 3 minutes. Turn the fish over and transfer to the preheated oven for a further 2 minutes, or until the fish is cooked through.

To serve

7 Ladle a circle of romesco sauce onto a plate and place the fish in the middle. Arrange the wilted chard, roasted potato and fennel alongside.

Omit the potatoes for a low-carb, keto-friendly weeknight meal. Leftover romesco sauce can be used on sandwiches, pasta or to add flavour to your morning scrambled eggs.

RUSTIC FISH COOKED IN BANANA LEAF

Cooking in a banana leaf gives an exceptional smoky quality and a succulent texture to the fish in this delectable recipe. The combination of spices, tamarind, coconut milk and coconut milk and butternut squash works splendidly with the fish.

350g fish fillet
2 x 30cm square pieces of banana leaves*
a marble-sized piece of compressed tamarind
1 small pink shallot
1 red chilli
1 clove garlic
1cm piece ginger
4 Tbsp freshly grated coconut
3 Tbsp water
1 tsp cumin seeds
¼ tsp black peppercorns
⅛ tsp mustard seeds
salt to taste
2 Tbsp coriander leaves, chopped
200g butternut squash
lime wedges to serve
*If fresh are unavailable, use frozen banana leaves, available from Asian supermarkets.

SERVES 2
PREP 30 MINS
+ MARINATING
COOKING 45 MINS

1 Powder the cumin, peppercorns and mustard seeds using a mortar and pestle or a grinder. Peel the ginger and garlic and process with the ground spices, coriander leaves, salt and chilli into a coarse paste.

2 Soak the tamarind with 1 Tbsp of water. Squeeze to extract the pulp, discard the membranes and seeds. Set aside until required.

3 Cut the fish into two pieces and transfer to a bowl with the spice paste and tamarind pulp. Massage well to coat and set aside in the refrigerator for 1–2 hours.

4 Preheat the oven to 180°C. Line a baking sheet with baking paper.

5 Wash the banana leaves under running water. To make them more pliable, dip the leaves in a bowl of hot water. Wash thoroughly and wipe them dry before using.

6 Peel and slice the butternut squash into ½cm thick slices. Place half the squash in the centre of each banana leaf. Lay a piece of spice-coated fish fillet on top. Fold each leaf into a parcel, securing with toothpicks or kitchen twine.

7 Arrange both fish parcels on the lined baking tray and transfer to the hot oven. Cook for 28–30 minutes. Remove from the oven.

8 Just before serving, open the parcels slightly. Garnish with extra coriander leaves and thinly sliced red chilli. Serve with some lime wedges on the side.

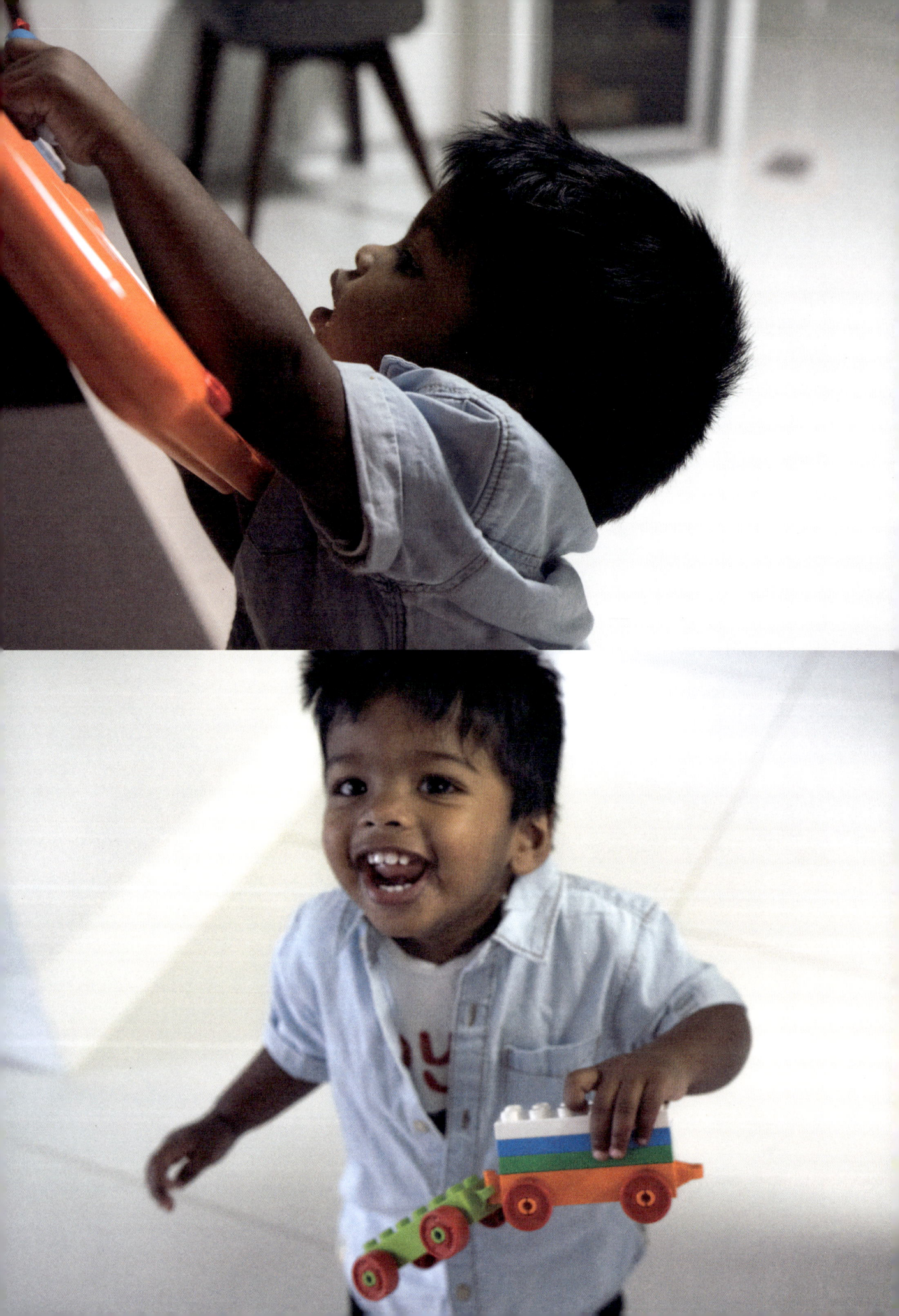

CABBAGE W/ PRAWNS

The gentle, earthy flavour of cabbage pairs admirably with ginger, garlic and prawns. A quick and easy side dish that you will find yourself returning to again and again.

1 cup prawns, shelled and cleaned
400g green cabbage
1½ Tbsp oil
1 medium onion, finely chopped
1 tsp ginger, grated
2 green chillies, sliced
1 clove garlic, minced
½ cup freshly grated coconut
1 tsp mustard seeds
½ tsp turmeric powder
salt to taste

SERVES 4
PREP 30 MINS
COOKING 30 MINS

1. Shred the cabbage into thin ribbons, wash and drain in a colander.

1. Heat the oil in a deep pan, add the mustard seeds and when they start to sputter, stir in the ginger, garlic, onion, curry leaves and green chillies. Sauté over a medium heat.

3. When the onion mixture turns golden and fragrant, add the coconut and fry for 1 minute.

4. Stir in the cabbage with salt and cook over a low heat for 5–10 minutes. Continue to stir the mixture making sure it doesn't burn.

5. Add the prawns and heat for another 4–5 minutes, until the prawns are cooked.

6. Serve with curry, rice and chapati.

KING PRAWNS + SCALLOPS W/ CRISPY KUMARA + CHUNKY RELISH

Sweet and succulent shellfish is delicately flavoured and paired with a tangy tomato relish and pan-fried kumara in this dazzling dish.

12 medium king prawns
12 scallops
4 tsp fennel seeds
1 tsp nigella seeds
¼ of a star anise
6 Tbsp rice bran oil
2 tsp chilli powder
4 garlic cloves, minced
2 tsp lime juice
salt to taste
1 Tbsp oil

For the relish

2 large ripe tomatoes
4 tsp extra virgin olive oil
½ cup red onions, diced
6 garlic cloves, minced
3 Tbsp caster sugar
3 Tbsp white vinegar
1 cup water
2 tsp mustard powder, freshly ground
salt to taste

For the pan-fried kumara

2 white kumara (about 600g)
rice bran oil for pan frying
½ tsp minced garlic
salt to taste

For garnish

chives batons

SERVES 4–6
PREP 30 MINS
COOKING 45 MINS

1 Wash and devein the prawns, leaving the tails and shells intact.

2 Using a dry grinder, powder the fennel, nigella seeds and star anise. Place the ground spice, oil, chilli powder, garlic, lime juice and salt in a bowl and mix to combine. Use this mixture to marinate the prawns and scallops. Set aside until required.

To make the relish

3 Prepare the tomatoes by blanching in boiling water for 1 minute. Transfer the tomatoes to a bowl and set aside to cool. Peel off the skin and dice into small cubes.

4 Heat the olive oil in a saucepan and sauté the onions and garlic. Add the diced tomatoes and cook for 2–3 minutes until soft. Add the sugar, vinegar, water and mustard powder, and cook over a low heat for 15–20 minutes or until soft. Remove from the heat and set aside to cool.

To cook the kumara

5 Peel and dice the kumara into small cubes and rub with salt and garlic. Heat the oil in a frying pan. Shallow fry the kumara until golden around the edges and cooked. Transfer to a dish and keep warm.

6 Preheat the frying pan to a high heat. Drizzle with oil and cook the prawns for 3–4 minutes each side until lightly browned. Remove, set aside, and keep warm. Using the same pan, sear the scallops, 1 minute each side until golden brown.

7 Serve the cooked prawns and scallops on a warmed plate with pan-fried kumara cubes and tomato relish. Garnish with chive batons.

SALMON W/ PUMPKIN PURÉE + TOASTED CUMIN + RELISH

This gorgeous New Zealand salmon and pumpkin recipe is remarkably easy to make and demonstrates my take on fusion flavours. The unusual pairing of curry powder, toasted cumin, mustard, parsley and relish transforms this dish into a magnificent starter or main.

750g salmon fillets (4 pieces)
1–2 tsp curry powder
2 tsp cumin seeds
salt to taste
2–3 tsp olive oil or oil spray

For the pumpkin purée
400g pumpkin
1½–2 cups stock or water
3 garlic cloves, crushed
2 Tbsp low fat cream cheese
¼ tsp white mustard seeds, powdered
salt to taste

For the tomato relish
2 large ripe tomatoes, diced
1 cup parsley, chopped
½ cup red onion, finely chopped
1 gherkin, finely chopped
1 Tbsp capers, chopped
3 tsp extra virgin olive oil
salt to taste
2 tsp lemon juice
2 tsp sugar or natural sweetener

For the garnish
2 tsp cumin seeds, toasted
12–15 chives, cut into long batons
micro cress

SERVES 4
PREP 30 MINS
COOKING 30 MINS

To make the tomato relish

1. Mix all the ingredients in a bowl. Cover with cling wrap and refrigerate.

To make the pumpkin purée

2. Peel and cut the pumpkin into 4cm chunks. Boil with salt, garlic and stock for 15–20 minutes or until soft.

3. Remove from the heat and put in the food processor with the rest of the ingredients, except the mustard powder. Process into a purée. Add the mustard powder and mix well. Transfer to a bowl and keep warm.

To cook the salmon

4. Place the salmon fillets on a lined baking tray. Brush the fish generously with olive oil and sprinkle with salt and curry powder. Set aside. Preheat the oven grill to 220°C.

5. Scatter the cumin seeds over the fillets and place under the grill, skin side up. Grill for 8–10 minutes, or until the salmon is cooked.

To serve

6. Pipe the pumpkin purée on each plate and spoon on some tomato relish. Place the grilled fish and scatter the toasted cumin seeds around. Garnish with chives batons and micro cress.

 Your best bet is to play on the freshness of the tomatoes in this otherwise rich dish. We suggest a Sparkling Champagne Rosé as it carries a bit more fruit, which will balance the spices better than a standard Champagne. The acidity will cut through the richness of the salmon and pumpkin, bringing everything to life.

CRAYFISH TAILS IN RED CURRY SAUCE W/ MANGO SAMBAL + GRATED COCONUT RICE

A fusion of aromatic flavours with sweetness from the firm, rich flesh of New Zealand's spiny rock lobster. Whether you plan to serve this dish for a romantic dinner or a posh dinner party with your friends, this recipe ticks all the boxes.

900g–1kg fresh crayfish tails

For the mango sambal
1 cup green sour mango, grated
1 cup coconut, freshly grated
3 medium pink shallots, finely chopped
1 red chilli, finely sliced
1 green chilli, finely sliced
10 curry leaves, sliced into thin ribbons
1 tsp ginger, freshly grated
salt to taste

For the grated coconut rice
1½ cups cooked basmati rice
¾ cup coconut, freshly grated
1 tsp butter
1 tsp cumin seeds
1 dried red chilli, torn into pieces
a sprig of curry leaves
salt to taste
a pinch of asafoetida

For the mango sambal
1. Place all the ingredients in a bowl and mix well to combine. Cover with cling wrap and set aside in the refrigerator.

For the coconut rice
2. Melt the butter in a pan and fry the mustard and cumin seeds until they sputter. Add the dried chillies and curry leaves, and fry for 2 minutes.

3. Add the asafoetida and grated coconut. Cook over a medium heat for 4–6 minutes until the mixture is lightly golden and fragrant. Incorporate the cooked rice and salt, and stir fry for 1 minute until combined. Remove from the heat and keep warm until required.

For the crayfish
4. Drop the crayfish tails into boiling water for 2 minutes, then refresh in iced water. Carefully remove the meat from the shells and slice into 5cm pieces. Trim the tails neatly and reserve the shells for presentation.

For the red curry sauce

- 3 medium pink shallots
- 3 cloves of garlic
- 3cm piece of ginger
- 3-4 long red chillies
- 2 tsp coriander seeds
- 2 tsp cumin seeds
- 1 tsp fennel seeds
- 1 Tbsp oil
- 1 tsp of garam masala powder*
- ½ tsp turmeric powder
- 2 ripe tomatoes, diced
- 1 ripe persimmon
- 1 cup coconut milk
- 1 cup water
- salt to taste
- 1 tsp butter
- a sprig curry leaves

For garnish

- a sprig of curry leaves
- fresh coriander leaves

*Refer to Spice Blends chapter

SERVES 2–4
PREP 45 MINS
COOKING 90 MINS

For the red curry sauce

5 Place the shallots, garlic, ginger, coriander chillies, cumin and fennel seeds with 2 Tbsp of water in a blender and process into a smooth paste.

7 Heat the oil in a large pan. Add the garam masala and fry for 15–20 seconds. Then add the turmeric and ground spice paste and fry for 5 minutes until aromatic.

8 Blend the tomatoes and persimmon in a food processor. Add the tomato mixture to the pan of spices, salt and cover with a lid and continue to cook over a gentle heat for 6–8 minutes.

9 Add the coconut milk and water and continue to simmer for 10 minutes. Then transfer the reserved shells into this sauce and continue to cook for a further 15 minutes.

10 Add the sliced crayfish meat into the curry sauce and cook for 6–10 minutes. Remove from the heat. Take the shells from the sauce and set aside, keeping them warm.

11 Lightly fry the sprig of curry leaves in 1 tsp of melted butter and add to the curry sauce.

To serve

12 Place the reserved shells onto plates and carefully pack them with the crayfish curry. Serve with coconut rice and mango sambal. Garnish with curry leaves and coriander.

CRAYFISH TAILS IN RED CURRY SAUCE, PAGE 158.

COD WITH ROMESCO SAUCE, PAGE 148

SNAPPER EN PAPILLOTE

En papillote is a superb French technique to cook food in a parcel. The fish steams in its juices, adding extra flavour and giving a tender result. I like to use instant white miso soup with tofu for this recipe. Its gentle, slightly sweet aroma adds a distinctive layer with unusual bursts of flavour.

450g snapper (scaled, gutted with head removed)
1 Tbsp good quality instant miso soup or white miso paste
1 clove garlic
3cm piece ginger
1–2 dried red chillies
2 Tbsp fresh lime juice
1 tsp peanut oil
2–3 Tbsp spring onions, sliced
1 Tbsp coriander leaves, chopped
salt to taste

SERVES 2
PREP 30 MINS
COOKING 30 MINS

1 In a food processor, process the instant miso soup, garlic, ginger and chilli to a coarse paste. Transfer to a bowl and mix with lime juice and peanut oil.

2 Place the fish in a wide dish and rub with the miso mixture, scatter with half of the chopped spring onions and coriander leaves.

3 Cut pieces of baking paper and aluminium foil large enough to wrap around the fish. Arrange the baking paper on the foil and place the fish in the middle. Fold and tightly seal the parcel, making sure there is adequate space for the steam to circulate and cook the fish. Set aside in the refrigerator for 2–3 hours for the flavours to develop.

4 Preheat the oven to 180–200°C. Place the fish parcel on a baking tray and bake for 25–30 minutes, or until the fish is cooked through.

5 Remove from the heat and open the parcel with care. Garnish the fish with the remaining spring onions and coriander leaves.

A healthy and delicious way to serve this fish is over a bed of blanched broccoli florets and sliced peppers, with lime wedges on the side.

PAN-DRESSED FISH W/ CHILLI + CORIANDER + TOMATO

This impressive fish recipe can be rustled up with minimal effort and makes a weeknight dinner a breeze. I choose this simple dish during the summer when lighter meals are favoured and snapper is readily available.

500g snapper (scaled, gutted with head and tail removed)
2 Tbsp olive oil
salt to taste
½ cup fresh coriander leaves, chopped, plus extra for garnish
1–2 tsp chilli flakes
½ tsp fresh ginger, grated
1 clove of garlic, peeled and finely chopped
3–4 Tbsp lime juice
½–¾ cup fresh tomatoes, diced
½ cup spring onions, chopped, plus extra for garnish

SERVES 2
PREP 30 MINS
COOKING 30 MINS

1. Preheat the oven to 180°C. Line a baking tray with foil and a layer of baking paper.

2. Rub the fish with olive oil, salt, coriander, chilli, garlic, ginger and lime juice, and place in the middle of the baking tray.

3. Arrange the diced tomatoes around the fish. Scatter the chopped spring onions over and around the fish.

4. Bake the fish for 15–20 minutes, or until it is cooked through.

5. Change the oven setting to grill and cook the fish for a further 8–10 minutes until it is nicely coloured.

6. Garnish with chopped coriander leaves and spring onions. Serve with rice noodles and salad of your choice.

MUM'S PRAWN FRIED RICE

My mother made this delicious prawn fried rice for family gatherings and served it with her expertly planned curry dishes. Leftovers are perfect for packed lunches and the glorious aroma often attracts compliments from workmates.

3 cups cooked rice
1 cup prawns or shrimps
8cm piece of pandan leaf
1½ cups carrots, julienned
1 small leek
¾ cup potatoes, julienned
1 pink shallot, sliced thinly
3 Tbsp rice bran oil
salt to taste
1–2 tsp chilli flakes
1 tsp vinegar

SERVES 4–6
PREP 30 MINS
COOKING 30 MINS

1. Rinse the leeks thoroughly under running water. Remove the root end, cut it lengthwise and slice thinly.

2. Heat 2 Tbsps of oil in a large frying pan and stir fry the julienned carrots, pandan leaves and potatoes. Sprinkle with salt.

3. When the carrots and potatoes are cooked halfway through, add the sliced shallot and leek, and continue to stir fry until the carrots turn golden around the edges. Remove from the heat.

4. In a separate pan, heat the remaining oil and stir fry the prawns with the chilli flakes. Add a pinch of salt and cook for 3–4 minutes. Place the cooked prawns in with the stir fried vegetables and mix in the vinegar.

5. Stir in the cooked rice and toss well to combine. Serve hot with your favourite relishes on the side.

SALADS
+
VEGES

THERE IS NOTHING MORE SATISFYING THAN A FRESH, HEALTHY SALAD MADE WITH SEASONAL PRODUCE.

TOP: JAFFNA CARROT SALAD, PAGE 174. BOTTOM: GOTU KOLA SALSA, PAGE 175

KALE VARAI

My love affair with kale started in 2005, a few years after the Otago Farmers Market was established in Dunedin. A renowned superfood, kale is healthy, delicious and so versatile that it can be used in a variety of dishes. Vegan, gluten-free and keto-friendly, this is a winning side dish that everyone can enjoy.

250g kale, rinsed and thinly shredded*
½ tsp turmeric powder
1 tsp roasted fennel powder**
¼ cup freshly grated coconut
3 tsp oil
1 tsp of mustard seeds
½ tsp cumin seeds
½ tsp fennel seeds
1 onion, diced finely
a sprig of curry leaves
1 green chilli, sliced
salt to taste

Either curly kale or cavolo nero (Tuscan kale) can be used for this recipe.
** Refer to recipe under Spice Blend section.

SERVES 4
PREP 30 MINS
COOKING 30 MINS

1. Place the shredded kale, turmeric, roasted fennel powder and coconut in a bowl and mix well to combine.

2. Heat the oil in a pan and fry the mustard, cumin and fennel seeds. When the mustard seeds start to sputter, add the diced onion, curry leaves and chillies, and sauté for a minute until the onion mixture is lightly coloured.

3. Stir in the kale mixture, cover and cook over a medium heat for 3 minutes. Remove the lid and stir fry for further 4–5 minutes until cooked but still firm to the bite.

4. Add the salt, stir well and remove from the heat. Serve with rice and curries.

JAFFNA CARROT SALAD

Mum always makes this on vegetarian days and I am still following her tradition! The sweetness of the carrots and coconut combined with tangy lime juice and zingy ginger make it a delicious, well-balanced side dish.

2 cups carrots, grated or julienned
2–3 Tbsp coconut, freshly grated
2 green chillies
1 red onion
4–5 curry leaves
1cm piece of ginger, finely grated
½ tsp freshly ground black pepper
juice of ½ a lime
salt to taste

SERVES 4
PREP 30 MINS

1. Finely chop the onions, curry leaves and green chilli, and mix with the carrots.

2. Stir in the ginger, salt and coconut.

3. Squeeze in the lime juice and mix well to combine. Cover and refrigerate until ready to serve.

BOILED EGG + RED ONION SALAD W/ COCONUT DRESSING

My father came up with the idea of this beautiful egg salad. It has now become one of our family's signature side dishes.

6 hard boiled eggs
1 large red onion
½ cup coconut milk
2 green chillies
4–5 curry leaves
1 lime
salt to taste
freshly ground black pepper to taste

SERVES 4–6
PREP 30 MINS

1. Peel the eggs and cut them lengthwise. Arrange on a serving dish.

2. Peel the onions and slice thinly. Transfer to a bowl.

3. Slice the green chillies diagonally and curry leaves into thin ribbons. Transfer to the bowl with the sliced onions.

4. Add salt, lime juice and coconut milk and gently crush and mix with your fingers.

5. Spread this onion and coconut milk mixture over the sliced eggs. Sprinkle generously with freshly ground black pepper. Serve this salad with rice, puttu, string hoppers and curries.

GOTU KOLA SALSA

The gotu kola plant grows in swampy areas in the tropics and also very well in Australia and New Zealand. It is available at most Asian greengrocers. In Sri Lankan culture, a popular belief is that gotu kala improves memory! My grandmother often encouraged us to eat this "brain food".

1 bunch of gotu kola
4–5 curry leaves
½ red onion
1 green chilli
2 Tbsp fresh grated coconut
salt to taste
juice of ½ a lime

SERVES 4
PREP 15 MINS

1. Wash the gotu kola leaves and stems and drain in a colander.

2. Take a handful of leaves including the stems, roll firmly like a cigar and shred finely. Place in a bowl. (One regular bunch should yield two cups once shredded.)

3. Shred the curry leaves, dice the onion, finely slice the chillies and transfer to the same bowl.

4. Add the coconut, salt and lime juice, and mix well to combine. Serve with rice and curries.

TOMATO W/ COCONUT + LIME DRESSING

Tomato salsa is an all-time favourite served with meat curry in most Sri Lankan households.

2 large ripe tomatoes
1 medium red onion
6–8 curry leaves
1–2 green chillies
6 Tbsp coconut milk
2 Tbsp lime juice
freshly ground black pepper
salt to taste

SERVES 4–6
PREP 30 MINS

1. Wash and dice the tomatoes into small pieces (about 1cm). Transfer to a serving bowl.

2. Finely chop the onions, curry leaves and green chillies, and add to the tomato mixture.

3. Add the coconut milk, black pepper, salt and lime juice, and mix well to combine. Refrigerate until ready to serve.

BOILED EGG + RED ONION SALAD, PAGE 174.

GOTU KOLA SALSA, PAGE 175.

COURGETTES IN YOGHURT SAUCE

Courgettes are in abundance at our local farmers' market during the summer. I add the crunch of fried dal, green chillies and the creaminess of yoghurt to create a well-balanced delightful dish.

450g courgettes
300ml natural yoghurt
1 tsp turmeric powder
salt to taste
½ cup water
1½ Tbsp oil
½ tsp mustard seeds
½ tsp cumin seeds
½ tsp chana dal
½ tsp urad dal
2cm ginger, minced
3–4 green chillies
1 sprig of curry leaves
¼ cup coriander leaves, chopped
¼ tsp cumin, freshly ground

SERVES 4
PREP 30 MINS
COOKING 30 MINS

1 Wash and cut the courgettes into thick half-moons. Place in a saucepan and boil with the turmeric, salt and water for 6–7 minutes. Remove from the heat and set aside.

2 Heat a pan with oil and fry the mustard and cumin seeds. As the seeds begin to sputter, add chana and urad dal, and fry until golden.

3 Stir in the green chillies and curry leaves and sauté for 2 minutes. Pour in the yoghurt and add the coriander leaves.

4 Remove from the heat and incorporate the boiled courgettes and cumin powder. Stir well to combine. Serve warm with rice, lentil curry and papadums.

ROASTED CORN + LEAFY GREENS W/ MISO DRESSING

I created this fresh, summery salad that makes the most of the new season veges. So gratifying on its own or works perfectly as a starter.

1 corn cob, husks and fibres removed
150g mesclun salad greens
1 Tbsp vegetable oil
1–2 baby carrots
4–5 small radishes
1 pink shallot, thinly sliced
2 tsp chilli flakes (optional)

For the miso dressing
1 tsp white miso paste
1 tsp fresh lemon juice
1 Tbsp mandarin juice
1 tsp mirin
1 tsp soy sauce
½ tsp pomegranate molasses
⅛ tsp ginger, finely minced
⅛ tsp garlic, finely minced
sea salt to taste

SERVES 2–4
PREP 30 MINS
COOKING 30 MINS

To make the dressing
1. Place the ingredients in a jar and shake well to combine. Set aside.

To cook the corn
2. Preheat a grill pan until hot. Brush the corn cob with ½ a Tbsp of oil and place onto the hot grill. Keep rotating every couple of minutes until it is slightly charred and cooked through. Wrap in foil and set aside to cool a little. Slice the kernels from the cob.

To assemble
3. Rinse the salad greens and spin until dry. Wash the carrots and radishes. Shave the baby carrots into thin ribbons using a peeler. Thinly slice the radishes.

4. Place the salad greens in a bowl and gently toss with remaining oil. Assemble the sliced radish, carrot ribbons, shallot and corn kernels with the greens.

5. Just before serving, drizzle dressing generously over the salad. Serve with a scattering of chilli flakes for an extra kick.

BROCCOLI SALAD W/ LIME + ORANGE VINAIGRETTE

Dressed with a sweet and sharp vinaigrette, this broccoli salad is an ideal companion to rich, spicy food and makes a great addition to any summer buffet.

3 cups broccoli florets
½ cup red onion, sliced
½ cup red and green pepper, sliced
200g mixed coloured cherry tomatoes
8–10 cashew nuts, lightly toasted

For the vinaigrette
½ cup fresh orange juice
1 Tbsp of orange zest
2 Tbsp fresh lime juice
1 Tbsp of lime zest
2 Tbsp olive oil
freshly ground pepper
salt to taste
½ tsp sugar
¼ tsp garlic, freshly minced

SERVES 4
PREP 30 MINS
COOKING 5 MINS

To cook the broccoli
1. Wash, then place the broccoli florets in salted boiling water for 2–3 minutes. The broccoli should be slightly softened but still bright green and firm.

2. Drain the hot water and place the broccoli in a bowl of ice water for 30 seconds.

3. Strain in a colander and set aside.

To make the vinaigrette
4. Place the oil, salt, pepper, sugar, minced garlic, orange and lime juices and zests in a bowl. Whisk until combined.

To serve
5. In a serving dish, arrange the broccoli florets, onion slices, sliced pepper, tomatoes and cashew nuts.

6. Drizzle with the vinaigrette and toss well before serving.

QUINOA APRICOT SALAD W/ PIQUANT DRESSING

I use black quinoa for this salad as it has more crunch than other types. This healthy salad with a tart cider dressing, makes an excellent lunch box option. It also pairs well with grilled meat or seafood.

½ cup black quinoa
2 apricots, cut into segments
100g courgette
150g mixed peppers
100g beetroot
75g carrots
3 tsp olive oil
1 clove of garlic, minced
1 tsp oak smoked salt
2 tsp cumin seeds
1½–2 cups vegetable stock or water
2 bay leaves
½ cup chopped parsley
¼ cup pistachios, toasted
mint leaves for garnish

For the dressing
¼ cup cider vinegar
4 tsp canola oil
½ tsp curry powder
1 tsp sugar
salt to taste

SERVES 2–4
PREP 30 MINS
COOKING 30 MINS

1. Prepare and cut the vegetables into similar-sized pieces. Combine the olive oil, garlic, salt and cumin seeds, and mix with the vegetables. Use ordinary salt if oak smoked salt is unavailable.

2. Place the vegetables on a tray and roast under a hot grill for 20–25 minutes until lightly golden. Remove from the oven and transfer to a bowl.

3. Boil the quinoa with vegetable stock and bay leaves for 28–30 minutes, or until cooked and the liquid is absorbed. Transfer to a bowl with the roasted vegetables.

To make the dressing

4. Heat the oil in a pan, add the curry powder and sizzle for 45 seconds. Remove from the heat and add the cider vinegar, salt and sugar, and stir well to combine.

To assemble

5. Add the dressing and chopped parsley with the quinoa mixture and gently stir to combine. Sprinkle with nuts and mint leaves. Arrange the apricot segments on top and serve.

BEETROOT + SPINACH SALAD W/ CREAMY CHILLI FETA DRESSING

A sensational and vibrant salad that delivers sweetness, sourness, saltiness and a touch of bitterness on one plate. A scattering of my crunch 'n' spice mix adds a bit of texture to create an entirely satisfying salad.

350g candy beetroot or regular beetroot
250g baby spinach leaves
1 red onion, sliced
2 Tbsp extra virgin olive oil

For the feta dressing
200g soft feta cheese
1 red chilli
1 tsp pomegranate molasses
1 clove of garlic

For the garnish
½ cup crunch 'n' spice mixture* or toasted walnuts
a handful of mint leaves
*Refer to page 62

SERVES 4
PREP 30 MINS
COOKING 60 MINS

1 Preheat the oven to 180°C.

2 Wash and dry the beetroot and wrap in foil. Bake for 1 hour.

To make the dressing
3 Place the feta, chilli, pomegranate molasses and garlic in a food processor and blend to a smooth sauce. Refrigerate for at least an hour for the flavours to develop.

To assemble
4 Remove the beetroot from the oven set aside for 15 minutes to cool. Trim and peel the beetroot, cut into wedges and transfer to a mixing bowl.

5 Mix the sliced onions and spinach leaves in with the beetroot, drizzle with the olive oil and toss to combine.

6 Spoon the dressing over the salad, sprinkle with crunch 'n' spice mixture or toasted nuts and serve.

EGGPLANT W/ ROASTED PEPPERS + CHICKPEA SALAD

This healthy salad is very simple to prepare and makes a wonderful vegetarian starter.

300g eggplant
200g red pepper
1 cup cooked chickpeas
2 Tbsp olive oil
1 tsp nigella seeds
1 tsp oak smoked salt
1 medium red onion, sliced
1 red chilli, finely chopped
½ cup flat leaf parsley, chopped
½ cup coriander leaves, chopped

For the dressing
zest of 1 lemon
juice of 1 lemon
4 Tbsp of extra virgin olive oil
1 tsp oak smoked salt
freshly ground black pepper
salt to taste

SERVES 4
PREP 30 MINS
COOKING 30 MINS

1 Preheat the oven to 180°C.

2 Wash and cut the eggplant into 1cm thick slices. Chop the red peppers into bite sized chunks. Place the cut vegetables in a bowl, add the oil, nigella seeds, smoked salt and mix well to combine. Spread evenly on a lined tray and bake for 25–30 minutes.

To make the dressing
3 Place all the ingredients except the olive oil in a bowl. Slowly incorporate the oil while whisking.

To assemble
4 In a separate bowl, place the chickpeas, sliced onions, chilli, chopped parsley, coriander leaves, and roasted vegetables. Pour in the dressing and toss well to combine.

KALE VARAI, PAGE 173 AND BEETROOT + SPINACH SALAD, PAGE 186

EGGPLANT WITH ROASTED PEPPERS + CHICKPEA SALAD, PAGE 187.

GARLIC SPINACH MASH W/ LIME + COCONUT MILK

The very first dish that my mum taught me to cook was this spinach mash. Although I was not too enthusiastic about cooking it at the time, it has become one of my favourites. Incredibly simple to make, it is a tasty recipe to have on hand for vegetarian emergencies!

450g fresh spinach
4 Tbsp thick coconut milk
juice of ½ a lime
½ cup onions, finely chopped
1 green chilli, chopped
3 cloves of garlic, chopped
6–8 curry leaves
3 Tbsp water
salt to taste

1. Clean and rinse the spinach. Drain in a colander and roughly chop, including the stalks. Place the cut spinach, onions, chilli, garlic, curry leaves and water in a pan. Cook over a low heat for 7–8 minutes, with the lid on.

2. Remove from the heat and mash until smooth. Alternatively, use a food processor and blend.

4. Add salt, lime juice and coconut milk. Stir well to combine.

SERVES 4
PREP 30 MINS
COOKING 30 MINS

This mash is a great accompaniment to any curry, especially a lentil or seafood one. Try it with my lentil curry with fried onion garnish, page 256.

QUINOA TABBOULEH W/ POMEGRANATE SEEDS

Classic Mediterranean tabbouleh salad gets a makeover with superfoods quinoa and pomegranate in this recipe.

½ cup quinoa
1 pomegranate
1 clove of garlic, finely chopped
1 Tbsp extra virgin olive oil
1 medium tomato, diced
1 cup flat leaf parsley, finely chopped
½ cup mint leaves, finely chopped
1 spring onion, thinly sliced
freshly ground black pepper
1 green chilli, finely chopped
2 Tbsp fresh lemon juice
salt to taste

SERVES 4–6
PREP 30 MINS
COOKING 30 MINS

1 Boil the quinoa in lightly salted water following the instructions on the pack. Drain in a colander and rinse thoroughly under cold water to remove any trace of bitterness. Drain completely.

2 Cut the pomegranate in half and remove the seeds.

3 Transfer all the ingredients to a bowl with the quinoa and toss well to combine.

MEAT-FREE CURRIES, PAGE 234.

CURRIES

THIS SECTION FEATURES A RANGE OF DELECTABLE CURRIES—FROM THE TRADITIONAL RECIPES PASSED DOWN OVER GENERATIONS TO MY OWN MODERN CREATIONS.

AUNTIE'S PRAWN CURRY, PAGE 221.

TIPS FOR CURRIES BEFORE YOU BEGIN

Success in creating a great curry relies upon intricately combining chillies, spices and herbs, as well as balancing sweetness, acidity and saltiness with fresh ingredients.

The basis for any Sri Lankan Jaffna curry recipe is the curry powder, onion, sea salt, coconut and the curry leaves. Dried long red chillies, curry leaves, coriander, cumin, fennel, fenugreek seeds and black peppercorns are the most common whole spices used in making the Jaffna curry powder. Kashmiri chilli powder gives a dish a distinct bright colour without the harsh burn of too much chilli. I want everyone to experience the joy of a curry that does not give off overwhelming heat. Kashmiri chilli is my secret to creating visually appealing curries with balanced flavours.

In most cases, the coconut milk forms the base sauce. The proportion of souring agents such as tamarind or lime and levels of aromatic spices such as the cinnamon, cardamom, cloves, ginger, garlic, lemongrass and pandan leaves will depend on the recipe itself.

GRANDMA'S LAMB CURRY

This recipe was passed down from my grandmother to my mum and it is utterly delightful. Traditionally, my grandmother used goat meat and slow-cooked this dish. Although goat meat is not very popular in Western cuisine, it is eaten extensively in Sri Lanka. Lamb works perfectly well. This is my family's go-to curry for Sunday lunches.

500g lamb leg steaks (bones in)

salt to taste

3–4 tsp curry powder (Jaffna style)*

2 tsp dark-roasted aromatic spice powder*

½ cup thick coconut milk

1 large onion, roughly chopped

2 sprigs of curry leaves

½ tsp garlic, freshly minced

½ tsp ginger, freshly grated

2 green chillies, sliced

5cm piece pandan leaf

¾ cup water

1 tsp roasted fennel powder*

*Refer to Spice Blends chapter

SERVES 4
PREP 30 MINS
COOKING 90 MINS

1. Trim any visible fat from the lamb and dice into 2cm sized pieces. Retain the bones for extra flavour.

2. In a large bowl, rub the meat with salt, curry powder and dark-roasted spice powder, and leave for a couple of hours or overnight in the fridge.

3. In a heavy saucepan, heat the coconut milk over a low heat until it begins to release the oil.

4. Add the onion, 1 sprig of curry leaves, garlic, ginger, chilli and pandan leaf to the reduced coconut milk. Cook until the mixture is fragrant and begins to caramelise.

5. Add the marinated lamb pieces, cover and cook over a low heat for 15–18 minutes or until the meat starts to release the juices. As the curry begins to boil, steadily incorporate the water. Cover and cook over a low temperature for 1–1½ hours.

6. When each piece of meat is coated well with the thickened gravy, add the remaining curry leaves and remove from heat.

7. Sprinkle over the roasted fennel powder and stir to combine. Serve with rice and side dishes of your choice.

PORK CURRY

There is no better way to showcase New Zealand pork than this Sri Lankan-style curry. Pork is excellent for slow-cooking and also holds up well against a big combination of aromatic spices. I make extra so I have leftovers – this tastes great the next day!

1kg pork shoulder chops, diced
a lime-sized piece of compressed tamarind
¾ cup water
2 tsp ginger, minced
2 tsp garlic, minced
salt to taste
2 tsp white vinegar
2 tsp curry powder (Jaffna style)*
1 Tbsp dark roasted curry powder*
½ tsp chilli flakes or powder
½ tsp freshly ground black pepper
½ tsp freshly ground mustard
4–5 cardamom pods, bruised
4cm cinnamon stick, lightly bruised
4 cloves, bruised
1 large onion, diced
½–1 green chilli, sliced
1 sprig of curry leaves
¼ cup coconut milk
5cm piece pandan leaf
½ tsp roasted fennel powder*
*Refer to Spice Blends chapter

SERVES 6
PREP 30 MINS
+ MARINATING
COOKING 60 MINS

1 Soak the tamarind with ¼ cup water for a few minutes. Extract the tamarind pulp and discard the seeds and membranes.

2 In a bowl, mix the pork pieces with ginger, garlic, salt, tamarind pulp, vinegar, Jaffna curry powder, dark roasted curry powder, chilli flakes, pepper and mustard powder and massage with your fingers. Leave to marinate for 1–2 hours.

3 Place the marinated pork, cardamom, cloves, cinnamon, onion, green chillies and curry leaves in a saucepan. Cover and cook over a low heat.

4 After 15 minutes, add the coconut milk with the remaining water and allow the curry to simmer until the sauce thickens.

5 Continue cooking for 45–50 minutes over a low heat, stirring occasionally. The meat should be tender and the pieces coated with sauce.

6 Sprinkle with roasted fennel powder and mix well. Serve with rice and vegetables of your choice.

Due to the strong spices and umami flavours in this curry, it is best paired with a creamy, malty English ale like Green King Strong Suffolk Ale. Remove ale from the fridge and leave to sit at room temperature for 10–20 minutes before serving. This enhances the fruity flavours.

CHICKEN BIRIYANI

Traditionally served with hard boiled eggs and raita, I like to serve this spicy chicken biriyani with egg salad and minty coriander yoghurt, which add depth to this fabulous dish.

1kg chicken (mixture of thighs and legs)
12cm cinnamon quill
8 cardamom pods
12 cloves
6 black peppercorns
1 tsp fennel seeds
½ tsp cumin seeds
½ tsp coriander seeds
3 Tbsp butter
3 Tbsp rice bran oil
4 cloves garlic, minced
5cm piece ginger, minced
1 tsp turmeric powder
1 tsp chilli powder
1 cup onion, chopped
4 cups fresh mint leaves
1½ cups natural yoghurt
1 cup water
salt to taste
½ cup coriander leaves, chopped

For the rice
2 cup basmati rice (soaked, washed and drained well)
2–2½ cup hot water
½ tsp saffron, soaked in 3 Tbsp hot water
a pinch of salt

1. Dry grind the cinnamon, cardamom, cloves, peppercorns, fennel, coriander and cumin seeds to a powder.

2. Melt the butter with the rice bran oil in a large pan over a gentle heat. Add the powdered spices and fry for a few seconds, stirring constantly. When the spice mixture is highly aromatic, add the garlic, ginger, turmeric and chilli powder. Stir fry for a further 2–3 minutes.

3. Add the chopped onions and mint leaves and fry for 3–4 minutes or until the onion is soft and fragrant.

4. Add the chicken pieces and mix well to coat with the aromatic spices. Turn and heat through to seal on both sides.

5. Stir in the yoghurt 1 Tbsp at a time, allowing it to absorb before adding the next spoonful.

6. Add the salt and water and cover with a lid. Simmer until the gravy is very thick and chicken is cooked. Remove from the heat and add chopped coriander leaves. Set aside.

To cook the rice

7. In another saucepan, bring the rice to a quick boil with hot water and salt. Let it boil rapidly for 3 minutes, then remove from the heat.

8. Add the soaked saffron with liquid into the rice. Transfer this rice mixture to the pan with the prepared chicken. Stir well, cover and simmer for 15–20 minutes or until the rice is cooked. Fluff with a fork.

For the fried onion garnish

½ red onion, thinly sliced
1 Tbsp butter
½ cup sliced almonds
¼ cup cashew nuts
¼ cup raisins or sultanas

For the minty coriander yoghurt

1 cup natural yoghurt
¼ cup mint leaves, chopped
¼ cup coriander leaves, chopped
salt to taste

SERVES 4–6
PREP 45 MINS
COOKING 60 MINS

To make the onion garnish

9. Melt the butter in a frying pan and fry the sliced onions until golden. Stir in the almonds and cashews. Add the raisins and fry for 1 minute. Garnish the biriyani rice with this mixture.

To make the minty yoghurt

10. Make the minty yoghurt by mixing all the ingredients together in a bowl.

Try this with my egg and red onion salad recipe on page 174. This recipe also works well with lamb leg instead of chicken.

CHICKEN PIRATTAL

Pirattal is a traditional Sri Lankan dry curry dish made with meat or vegetables. Garlic, ginger and aromatic spices enhance the coconut base in this delicious chicken version.

450g boneless chicken, diced
salt to taste
1 tsp turmeric powder
3–4 tsp curry powder (Jaffna style)*
2 tsp dark-roasted aromatic spice powder*
¼ tsp mustard seeds
¼ tsp cumin seeds
1 large onion, roughly diced
2cm piece of ginger, grated
3 cloves garlic, minced
1 ripe tomato, diced
2 green chillies, sliced
2 sprigs of curry leaves
½ cup coconut milk
2 tsp oil
1 tsp roasted fennel powder*
*Refer to Spice Blends chapter

For the garnish
fried green chillies to taste
a sprig of curry leaves

SERVES 4
PREP 30 MINS
+ MARINATING
COOKING 45 MINS

1. Rub the chicken pieces with salt, turmeric, Jaffna curry powder and dark-roasted aromatic spice powders, and set aside for half an hour.

2. Heat the oil in a saucepan and fry the mustard and cumin seeds. When the seeds begin to sputter, add the ginger, garlic, onion, curry leaves and green chillies. Sauté over a medium heat.

3. When the onions turn translucent and lightly golden, add the diced tomato. Cover and cook for 2–3 minutes.

4. Add the marinated chicken pieces to the onion mixture, cover, and simmer for 8–10 minutes. The chicken will cook gently in its own juices.

5. Stir in the coconut milk and simmer over a low heat for 20–25 minutes or until chicken pieces are cooked through and coated with thickened sauce.

6. Remove from the heat and sprinkle in roasted fennel powder. Mix well. Garnish with fried chilli and curry leaves. Serve with rice, chapati or naan bread.

SPICY VENISON PIRATTAL

Vension is low in fat and rich in iron. I use wild New Zealand venison, which is very delicate and has exquisite texture. Cooking over a low temperature results in meltingly tender meat in this gourmet take on a classic pirattal.

450g lean venison, diced
salt to taste
1 tsp white vinegar
1 tsp chilli powder
3 tsp dark-roasted aromatic spice powder*
2 tsp oil
1 large onion, sliced
2 sprigs of curry leaves
½ tsp garlic, freshly minced
½ tsp ginger, freshly minced
2 green chillies, sliced
2 tsp curry powder (Jaffna style)*
½ cup light coconut milk
1 cup water
½ cup coriander leaves, chopped
1 tsp roasted fennel powder*
*Refer to Spice Blends chapter

1. In a large bowl, rub the meat pieces with salt, vinegar, chilli powder and dark-roasted spice powder. Set aside to marinate.

2. Heat the oil in a heavy-based pan and sauté onion, a sprig of curry leaves, garlic, ginger and green chillies until the onion begins to caramelise.

3. Add the curry powder and marinated venison to the onion mixture. Add the coconut milk. Cover and cook over a low heat.

4. As the curry begins to boil, incorporate the water. Cover and continue to cook over a low heat for 1–1½ hours, until the curry thickens considerably. The meat should be tender and coated nicely with the gravy.

5. Add the chopped coriander leaves and the second sprig of curry leaves. Remove the curry from the heat.

6. Sprinkle the roasted fennel powder and stir well to combine. Serve with rice and side dishes of your choice.

SERVES 4
PREP 30 MINS
+ MARINATING
COOKING 90 MINS

GREEN HERBAL CHICKEN CURRY

This delightful, punchy, herbal chicken curry is inspired by a similar dish served in Hyderabadi (Indian) restaurants. Green chillies and fresh herbs give the unique green colour and heavenly taste to this version.

1kg chicken cut into pieces (mixture of breast, legs and thighs)
salt to taste
½ tsp turmeric powder
2½ tsp cumin seeds
1 Tbsp coriander seeds
8–10 black peppercorns
3cm piece of ginger, sliced
5–6 garlic cloves
8–10 green chillies, sliced
2 tsp oil
1½ cups onions, diced
2 cups fenugreek leaves, chopped
½ cup coriander leaves, chopped
1 cup water
1 cup tomatoes, diced
juice of ½ a lime

SERVES 4–6
PREP 30 MINS + MARINATING
COOKING 45 MINS

1. Wash the chicken pieces and pat dry with a paper towel. Rub with salt and turmeric powder and set aside.

2. Grind the cumin seeds, coriander seeds and peppercorns to a powder. Add ginger, garlic and green chillies, and grind to a coarse paste.

3. Heat the oil in a saucepan and sauté the onions until lightly coloured and fragrant.

4. Add the spice paste and stir constantly, cooking for 2–3 minutes, or until the mixture is aromatic.

5. Add the chicken pieces, fenugreek leaves, coriander leaves and water. Cover and cook for 5–6 minutes, stirring occasionally.

6. Stir in the diced tomatoes, cover and cook for a further 5–6 minutes, or until the gravy is thick and the chicken pieces are coated with curry sauce.

7. Remove from the heat, add the lime juice and stir well. Serve with hot rice, chapati or naan bread.

MEEN CHARAKKU KULAMBU/FISH CURRY

My grandmother's classic fish recipe is simplicity itself. She used to make this curry with the freshly ground spice paste, prepared with whole ingredients. For a more authentic, unique flavour, I like to cook this curry in a traditional Sri Lankan clay pot.

600–750g snapper or kingfish (whole fish or fillets)
a golf ball-sized piece of compressed tamarind
1 cup water
salt to taste
1½ cups thick coconut milk
2 sprigs of curry leaves
¼ tsp turmeric powder
¼ tsp fenugreek seeds

For the spice paste
1½ Tbsp coriander seeds
1 Tbsp cumin seeds
½ tsp black peppercorns
3–4 cloves of garlic
2cm piece of ginger
2–4 fresh red chillies
3–4 curry leaves
1 large pink shallot

SERVES 4
PREP 30 MINS
COOKING 30 MINS

For the spice paste
1 Place the coriander, cumin and black pepper in a blender and grind to a fine powder. Add the garlic, ginger, curry leaves, shallots and chilli with a sprinkle of water and grind to a smooth paste.

To make the curry
2 In a bowl, soak the tamarind in water for 15 minutes. Reserve the tamarind water and discard the pulp, membranes and seeds.

3 Place the spice paste, tamarind water, salt, coconut milk, curry leaves, turmeric and fenugreek seeds in a saucepan and bring to the boil.

4 Cut the fish into chunks. If using a whole fish, the fish head can be incorporated into the curry, or cooked separately!

5 Add the fish to the saucepan and simmer for 10–12 minutes until the sauce thickens.

6 Serve this tasty curry with rice and vegetable side dishes of your choice.

MANGO CHICKEN CURRY

Sweet mango complements the aromatic spices in this delicious chicken curry. With its interplay of spicy, sweet and sharp flavours, mango chicken curry is an incredibly versatile and vibrant dish.

450g chicken, cut into pieces (or a mixture of legs and thighs)
1 medium mango, moderately ripe
1 tsp turmeric powder
½ tsp Kashmiri chilli powder
2 tsp curry powder (Jaffna style)*
salt to taste
1 tomato, diced
1 red onion, diced
3 cloves garlic, minced
2cm piece of ginger, grated
3 Tbsp oil
1 tsp Indian masala powder*
½ tsp cumin powder
½ tsp coriander powder
½ cup natural yoghurt
½ cup water
½ cup coriander leaves chopped
*Refer to Spice Blends chapter

SERVES 4
PREP 30 MINS
+ MARINATING
COOKING 45 MINS

1. Place the chicken pieces in a bowl with turmeric, Kashmiri chilli, curry powder and salt. Mix well to combine and set aside.

2. Peel and cut the mango into small chunks. Place in a food processor with the tomatoes, onion, garlic and ginger. Blend to a smooth purée.

3. Heat the oil in a saucepan and gently fry the Indian masala, cumin and coriander powders until aromatic.

4. Add the puréed mango mixture and cook over a high heat for 2–4 minutes.

5. Add the chicken pieces and cook over a medium-high heat for 10–15 minutes.

6. Gradually stir in the yoghurt and water and cook for 10–15 minutes, or until the chicken is cooked and coated with thickened sauce.

7. Garnish with chopped coriander leaves and diced mango pieces. Serve with rice or Indian flat bread.

AUNTIE'S PRAWN CURRY

My mouth still waters when I think about my auntie's spicy prawn curry. Juicy prawns coated in a thick warming sauce remind me of my childhood in Sri Lanka. Gentle heat from the spice balances brilliantly with the sweetness of creamy coconut milk and tangy tamarind. This curry is full of flavour and tastes even better the next day!

400g prawns, shelled and cleaned
a golf ball-sized piece of compressed tamarind
1 cup water
1 Tbsp oil
¼ tsp fenugreek seeds
¼ tsp cumin seeds
1 large onion, chopped
2 green chillies, sliced
6 cloves garlic, sliced
1 clove garlic, crushed
2cm piece ginger, minced
a sprig of curry leaves
1 tsp Kashmiri chilli powder
2 tsp curry powder (Jaffna style)*
1 tomato, diced
salt to taste
1 cup thick coconut milk
¼ tsp cumin, freshly ground
¼ tsp black pepper, freshly ground
*Refer to Spice Blends chapter

SERVES 4
PREP 30 MINS
COOKING 30 MINS

1. Soak the tamarind in water for a few minutes. Extract the tamarind pulp and discard the membranes and seeds.

2. In a large pan, heat the oil and fry the fenugreek and cumin seeds for 15–20 seconds. Add the onion, chillies, sliced garlic, ginger, and curry leaves and sauté for 5–6 minutes until the onion is soft and golden.

3. Stir in the prawns, chilli, curry powder, and tomato and cook for 3–4 minutes, until aromatic.

4. Add the salt, tamarind pulp and coconut milk and bring to a boil. Then reduce the heat and simmer for 18–20 minutes.

5. When the sauce has thickened, add the crushed garlic, freshly ground cumin and black pepper, and stir well to combine. Remove from the heat.

6. Serve with rice or Indian flat bread and side dishes of your choice.

CRAB CURRY

Crab is the star of this dish. Its natural flavour is not overpowered by the delicately spiced coconut and tamarind sauce. If you want to enjoy this beautiful crab curry entirely, then be prepared to get your fingers dirty!

4 medium-sized crabs
a golf ball-sized piece of compressed tamarind
1 cup water
1 Tbsp oil
¼ tsp mustard seeds
¼ tsp fennel seeds
¼ tsp cumin seeds
1 medium red onion, diced
2 tsp garlic, finely chopped
2 tsp ginger, finely chopped
1 green chilli, sliced
a sprig of curry leaves
½ tsp fenugreek seeds
3 tsp curry powder (Jaffna style)*
salt to taste
1 cup coconut cream
1 tsp roasted fennel powder*
juice of ½ a lime
*Refer to Spice Blends chapter

SERVES 4
PREP 30 MINS
COOKING 30 MINS

1. Rinse each crab under running water. Separate the top shell by forcing it away from the main body. Remove the gills and guts. Break each crab into two pieces along its centre line by pushing upwards with your thumbs in the middle and pulling both sides downwards.

2. In a bowl, soak the tamarind in water for 10 minutes. Extract the tamarind pulp and discard the membranes and seeds.

3. Heat the oil in a pan and fry the mustard, fennel and cumin seeds. Add the onion, garlic, ginger, chilli, curry leaves and fenugreek seeds and sauté until the mixture is lightly coloured and fragrant.

4. Stir in the curry powder and cook for 30 seconds. Add the salt, tamarind pulp and coconut cream, and bring to a boil. Cook for 5–6 minutes.

5. Add the crab pieces. Cover and simmer for 15–20 minutes, or until the sauce thickens. If the sauce is still too thin, remove the cooked crab pieces and set aside in a dish. Boil the remaining liquid until you achieve the desired thickness, and transfer the crab pieces back into the sauce.

6. Remove from the heat and sprinkle with roasted fennel powder. Add the lime juice and stir to combine. Serve with rice, puttu, string hoppers, or Indian flat bread.

JAFFNA CUTTLEFISH CURRY

This slow-cooked cuttlefish dish is extra spicy and is an antidote to wintry weather. If you are not a fan of fiery curry, then adjust the quantity of curry powder.

475–500g cuttlefish or squid
1 cup coconut milk
¼ cup water
3–4 pink shallots, chopped
2 cloves of garlic, minced
½ tsp fresh ginger, grated
2–4 tsp curry powder (Jaffna style)*
½ tsp turmeric powder
¼ tsp fenugreek seeds
2 green chillies, chopped
½ tsp mild Kashmiri chilli powder
2 sprigs of curry leaves
salt to taste
juice of ½ a lime
1 tsp roasted fennel powder*
*Refer to Spice Blends chapter

SERVES 4
PREP 30 MINS
COOKING 30 MINS

1. Wash the cuttlefish and cut into 2cm. Transfer to a saucepan.

2. Add all the ingredients to the diced cuttlefish except for the lime juice and roasted fennel powder. Combine well.

3. Cover and gently simmer over a low heat for 20–25 minutes, stirring every 10 minutes.

4. Remove from the heat when the cuttlefish is tender and each piece is coated well with the spicy sauce.

5. Add the lime juice and sprinkle with roasted fennel powder. Mix well.

6. Serve with rice or puttu and your choice of vegetable dishes.

JAFFNA CHICKEN CURRY

In our hometown of Jaffna, we made this curry with stewing chicken or roosters. Nowadays, I use free-range broiler chicken, which takes less time to cook. This is an impressive curry you will return to again and again.

1½ kg whole chicken
salt to taste
½ tsp Kashmiri chilli powder
½ tsp turmeric powder
2cm piece of ginger, minced
2 tsp garlic, minced
1 Tbsp curry powder (Jaffna style)*
½ tsp fenugreek seeds
2 tsp oil
1½ cups onions, diced
2 green chillies, sliced
a sprig of curry leaves
8cm piece pandan leaf
1 cup coconut milk
1 cup water
½ tsp roasted fennel powder*
juice of ½ a lime
*Refer to Spice Blends chapter

SERVES 4–6
PREP 30 MINS + MARINATING
COOKING 45 MINS

1. Remove the skin and cut the chicken into even-sized pieces. Reserve the bones for flavour. Rinse and pat dry with a paper towel.

2. Place the chicken pieces in a bowl. Mix with salt, chilli powder, turmeric, ginger, garlic, curry powder and fenugreek seeds, and massage well. Set aside for 20–25 minutes.

3. Heat the oil in a saucepan and sauté the onions, green chillies, curry leaves and pandan leaves. Cook until the mixture is lightly golden and fragrant.

4. Add the chicken pieces and bones to the onion mixture and cook for 2–3 minutes. Stir in the coconut milk with water, and cook over a medium heat for 18–25 minutes or until the chicken is cooked and nicely coated with the curry sauce.

5. Remove from the heat and add the roasted fennel powder and lime juice. Mix well and serve with rice, puttu, or string hoppers.

JAFFNA CUTTLEFISH CURRY, PAGE 224.

NETHILI PIRATTAL/DEVILLED ANCHOVIES

Dried anchovies or sprats are a traditional part of Sri Lankan cuisine as they provide an inexpensive source of protein. People seem to either love or hate these small dried fish. I find their saltiness contrasts well with spicy flavours.

100g dried anchovies or sprats
a marble-sized piece of compressed tamarind
¼ cup of water
3–4 Tbsp oil
1 large red onion, sliced
2 red chillies, sliced
a sprig of curry leaves
salt to taste
1 tsp turmeric powder
2 tsp curry powder
3 Tbsp coconut milk

SERVES 4
PREP 30 MINS
COOKING 30 MINS

1. Soak the tamarind with water in a bowl for a few minutes. Extract the pulp and discard the membranes and seeds. Set aside.

2. Soak the anchovies in warm water for 30 minutes. Drain and rinse thoroughly. Drain again.

3. Heat the oil in a frying pan and fry the anchovies for 6–7 minutes.

4. Add the onion, chillies and curry leaves, and cook over a low heat for a further 15–20 minutes until the anchovies turn golden brown.

5. Stir in the salt, turmeric and curry powder, and cook for 5 minutes or until aromatic.

6. Add the coconut milk and tamarind pulp, cover and cook until the mixture is relatively dry.

7. Serve with rice and seasonal vegetables.

SAUTÉED SALTED DRIED FISH + HOT CAPSICUM

Salted dried fish is a highly sought-after delicacy in Sri Lanka. It is used to enhance the flavour and piquancy of many dishes. Dried fish complements the hot banana chillies with its saltiness and punchy taste. The sweetness of the caramelised coconut milk balances the flavours.

150g salted dried fish

250g hot banana chillies or capsicum, thickly sliced

½ cup of thick coconut milk

1 large onion, sliced

a sprig of curry leaves

10cm piece of pandan leaf

½ tsp turmeric powder

½ tsp mixed allspice powder*

1 Tbsp curry powder (Jaffna style)*

salt to taste

*Refer to Spice Blends chapter

SERVES 4
PREP 30 MINS + SOAKING
COOKING 30 MINS

1 Soak the dried fish in warm water for 45 minutes. Discard the water and rinse the fish thoroughly to remove the excess salt.

2 Place a frying pan on the stove and heat the coconut milk steadily, until the milk caramelises and the oil starts to separate.

3 Combine the sliced onions, curry leaves and pandan leaf. Sauté for 10 minutes until the onion is translucent.

4 Add the dried fish, turmeric, allspice and curry powders, and stir fry for 2–3 minutes.

5 Add sliced capsicums, cover, and cook over a medium heat for 12–15 minutes, stirring occasionally until the mixture is fairly dry.

6 Do a taste test before adding any extra salt. Remove from the heat and serve with rice and curries of your choice.

SOTHI

This delicate coconut soup is a Sri Lankan favourite, usually served with rice or string hoppers. My guests enjoy drinking my shrimp and tomato sothi straight from a mug!

1½ cups coconut milk
10–12 shrimps with heads, cleaned
a walnut-sized piece of compressed tamarind
2–3 cups water
1 tomato cut into quarters
1–2 pink shallots, sliced
2 green chillies, sliced
¼ tsp fenugreek seeds
¼ tsp turmeric powder
a sprig of curry leaves plus extra for garnish
salt to taste

SERVES 4
PREP 30 MINS
COOKING 30 MINS

1. Using your fingers, roll the tamarind into a firm ball. Place it in a saucepan.

2. Add all the ingredients except the coconut milk. Bring to a boil. Then turn down the heat and simmer for 6–8 minutes, or until the onion and tomato soften.

3. Add the coconut milk and stir continuously for 2 minutes. Take care not let the mixture boil over!

4. Keeping the tamarind ball intact helps to control the acidity and colour of the broth. Be mindful not to break it up while stirring! Remove from heat and add extra curry leaves.

Fish and green mango variation

Leave out the tomato, tamarind and shrimp. Use diced green mangoes and pieces of fresh fish for a flavoursome broth. Boil all the the ingredients except the fish and coconut milk until the mangoes soften. Then add the fish and cook for a further 8–10 minutes. Add the coconut milk and curry leaves and stir continuously for 2 minutes. Remove from the heat and add extra curry leaves.

Tomato and lime variation

Use lime as the souring agent for this recipe. Place all the ingredients in a pot except the coconut milk and lime juice. Bring to a boil and cook until the onion and tomato soften. Add the coconut milk and stir continuously for 2 minutes. Squeeze in the lime juice and stir to combine.

MEAT-FREE CURRIES

COOKING MEAT-FREE DISHES AND ENTERTAINING VEGETARIAN GUESTS DOESN'T HAVE TO BE A CHALLENGE.

VEGETABLES CAN BE JUST AS EXCITING AS MEAT, IF NOT MORE SO!

OKRA + TOMATO CURRY, PAGE 248.

GRANDMA'S LEEK + POTATO VARAI

My paternal grandmother made this dish every time she visited from her village. I learned from her that leek tastes fabulous when cooked with a bit of melted butter or ghee. The mild sweetness of leek contrasts perfectly with the spices, while potato adds texture.

1 large leek
1 medium potato, boiled and cut into small cubes
2 tsp butter or ghee
1 tsp vegetable oil
½ tsp mustard seeds
½ tsp cumin seeds
½ tsp fennel seeds
½ cup onions, diced
a sprig of curry leaves
1 red or green chilli, sliced
½ cup freshly grated coconut
½ tsp turmeric powder
½ tsp chilli powder
½ tsp roasted fennel powder*
salt to taste
Refer to Spice Blends chapter

SERVES 4
PREP 30 MINS
COOKING 30 MINS

1. Rinse the leek thoroughly under running water. Remove the root ends and cut it in half lengthwise, then slice it thinly.

2. Heat a frying pan and melt the butter over a gentle heat. Add the vegetable oil and fry the mustard, cumin and fennel seeds. When the mustard seeds begin to sputter, add the onions, curry leaves and chilli. Sauté for 1–2 minutes until the onion mixture turns a light golden colour.

3. Stir in the sliced leek, salt, turmeric, chilli powder, coconut and potatoes. Cover and cook over a medium heat for 5–6 minutes.

4. Remove the lid and cook for a further 6–7 minutes, stirring occasionally to prevent the varai catching on the bottom of the pan. Remove from the heat and serve as a side dish with rice and curries.

We recommend a soft and fruity but dry Rosé, or a textural and smooth semi-dry white wine, like one from the Jura region in France (Chardonnay and Savagnin Blend), or Alsace Pinot Blanc.

CAULIFLOWER + TOMATO CURRY W/ SWEET POTATO

Two superfoods come together in this wonderful vegetable curry. Soft, baked sweet potato contrasts superbly with crunchy cauliflower and delicately spiced tomato sauce. My family and friends voted this the most delicious vegetarian creation from my kitchen!

1 medium head of cauliflower
200g sweet potatoes
400g can of tomatoes
2-3 Tbsp olive oil
1 clove of garlic, crushed
½ tsp chana dal
½ tsp mustard seeds
½ tsp cumin seeds
1 medium onion, sliced
1-2 green chillies, sliced
3cm piece ginger, grated
a sprig of curry leaves
1 tsp Indian masala powder*
½ tsp turmeric powder
½ tsp Kashmiri chilli powder
salt to taste
fresh coriander leaves to garnish
*Refer to Spice Blends chapter

SERVES 4-6
PREP 30 MINS
COOKING 45 MINS

1. Preheat the oven to 180°C. Wash and cut the cauliflower into florets. Peel, rinse and cut the sweet potatoes into cubes.

2. Place the sweet potatoes in a bowl with 1 Tbsp of olive oil and the crushed garlic. Mix well and spread on a lined baking tray. Bake for 25-30 minutes, or until tender and lightly golden around the edges. Remove from the oven and set aside.

3. In a pan, heat the remaining oil and fry the chana dal, mustard and cumin seeds until the seeds begin to sputter.

4. Add the onion, chillies, ginger and curry leaves and cook for 5-6 minutes, or until the onions become soft and translucent.

5. Stir in the masala, turmeric and Kashmiri chilli powders. Cook until the mixture is fragrant.

6. Add the cauliflower florets and salt, and stir fry over a high heat for 1 minute to coat the vegetables with aromatic spices. Mix in the baked sweet potatoes and canned tomatoes with juice. Boil for 15-18 minutes, or until the liquid is absorbed. The cauliflower should still hold its shape and be crunchy.

7. Remove from the heat, top with coriander leaves and serve with rice or chapati.

BRINJAL/EGGPLANT WHITE CURRY

Several generations of my family have enjoyed this essential side dish for lamb curries. Green chilli adds a bit of heat and the coconut milk beautifully balances this dish with its sweet, creamy taste.

500g long eggplants
¼ cup onions, chopped
1 green chilli
a sprig of curry leaves
salt to taste
a pinch of fenugreek seeds
1½ cups water
¼ cup thick coconut milk
2 tsp fresh lime juice

For the garnish
1 tsp oil
½ tsp mustard seeds
¼ tsp fennel seeds
¼ tsp cumin seeds
1 pink shallot, finely sliced
1 dried red chilli
8 curry leaves

SERVES 4
PREP 30 MINS
COOKING 30 MINS

1. Rinse and cut the eggplants into 2cm pieces. Place in a saucepan with the onions, chilli, curry leaves, salt, fenugreek seeds and water. Cover and simmer for 10–12 minutes.

2. Add the coconut milk and cook for 5–6 minutes. Remove from the heat and add the lime juice.

To prepare the garnish
3. Heat the oil in a frying pan and fry the seeds until they start to sputter. Add the shallot, chilli and curry leaves and fry for 2–4 minutes, until golden brown. Scatter the garnish over the eggplant curry and serve.

 This is best served as a side dish with meat curries. Try it with my grandma's lamb curry, page 202.

CHICKPEAS W/ SPINACH + RED PEPPERS

This vibrant dish has an enticing mixture of chickpeas, peppers and spinach in a delicious, aromatic sauce. It is a perfect accompaniment to Indian flatbreads or warm, crusty bread.

400g canned or cooked chickpeas, drained
2 cups baby spinach, rinsed
1 medium red pepper, diced
2 Tbsp olive oil
½ tsp mustard seeds
½ tsp cumin seeds
1 tsp garlic, minced
1 tsp ginger, minced
1 medium red onion, sliced
2 green chillies, sliced
a sprig of curry leaves
1 tsp garam masala powder*
1 tsp turmeric
1 tsp Kashmiri chilli powder
1 medium tomato, diced
salt to taste
1½ cups water
½ cup coconut milk
2 Tbsp coriander leaves, chopped

* Refer to Spice Blends section.

SERVES 4
PREP 30 MINS
COOKING 30 MINS

1. Heat the oil in a large saucepan and fry the mustard and cumin seeds until they begin to sputter.

2. Add minced garlic and ginger and stir fry for 30 seconds. Stir in the onion, chillies and curry leaves, and cook for 5–6 minutes, or until the onions become soft and translucent.

3. Stir in the garam masala, turmeric and Kashmiri chilli powders. Cook for 2–3 minutes, or until the mixture is fragrant.

4. Add the tomatoes, chickpeas, red pepper and salt. Stir fry over a medium-high heat for 1 minute.

5. Stir in the water and coconut milk. Bring to the boil and simmer for 20–25 minutes, or until the gravy thickens.

6. Add the spinach, cover and cook for 1–2 minutes. Remove from the heat.

7. Garnish with coriander leaves and serve with chapati or naan bread.

MORINGA/DRUMSTICK CURRY

The moringa (drumstick) plant thrives in Sri Lanka. Many Sri Lankans grow moringa at home. Used as the primary ingredient in many vegetarian recipes, this vegetable derives its name from its stick-like form. The long pods are cut into pieces before cooking and are an excellent source of dietary fibre.

450–500g moringa
1 Tbsp rice bran oil
½ tsp mustard seeds
¼ tsp cumin seeds
¼ tsp fennel seeds
¼ tsp fenugreek seed
1 onion, sliced
3 cloves of garlic, chopped
1–2 green chillies, sliced
a sprig of curry leaves, plus extra for garnish
2 tsp curry powder (Jaffna style)*
¾ tsp turmeric
salt to taste
¾ cup coconut milk
2 cups water
1 medium tomato, diced
150–200g potato, peeled and quartered

SERVES 4
PREP 30 MINS
COOKING 30 MINS

1 Prepare the drumsticks by gently scraping off the dark outer layer of skin. This process helps to remove bitterness. Cut the moringa into 8cm long pieces and split each piece in half. Wash, pat dry and set aside.

2 Heat the oil in a pan and lightly fry the mustard, cumin, fennel and fenugreek seeds. Add the onion, garlic, chilli, sprig of curry leaves and potato pieces and sauté for 4–5 minutes until golden.

3 Add the moringa pieces to the onion mixture and cook for 35–40 seconds.

4 Combine the curry powder, turmeric, salt, coconut milk and water and add to the moringa mixture. Cover and cook for 20–25 minutes, stirring occasionally.

5 Add the tomatoes and cook for a further 10–15 minutes or until the moringa and potatoes are tender and the gravy is thick. Remove from the heat.

6 Fry the extra curry leaves in a little oil or butter and garnish the curry. Serve with rice, puttu or naan bread.

BEETROOT CURRY

Beetroot might not scream 'curry' to everyone, but beetroot curry is a classic side dish in Sri Lanka. This recipe offers a beautiful blend of spicy, sweet, sharp and zesty. It will add vibrant colour and flavour to any meal.

650–750g beetroot
1 tsp oil
1 medium onion, chopped
½ tsp garlic, finely chopped
½ tsp ginger, finely chopped
1 green chilli, sliced
a sprig of curry leaves
¼ tsp fenugreek seeds
¼ tsp cumin seeds
½ tsp turmeric powder
salt to taste
1 tsp curry powder (Jaffna style)*
½ cup coconut milk
½ cup water
juice of ½ a lime
1 tsp roasted fennel powder*
*Refer to Spice Blends chapter

SERVES 4
PREP 30 MINS
COOKING 30 MINS

1. Peel the beetroot, rinse and cut into small, even-sized cubes.

2. Heat the oil in a pan, fry the onion, garlic, ginger, chilli, curry leaves, fenugreek and cumin seeds until the onion begins to colour.

3. Stir in the beetroot cubes, turmeric, salt and curry powder, and cook for 30 seconds, until the mixture is aromatic.

4. Add the water and coconut milk. Cover and cook for 25–30 minutes, or until the liquid is absorbed.

5. The softened beetroot should retain its shape and still be firm to the bite. Remove from the heat, stir in the fennel powder and lime juice. Mix well and serve.

I serve this curry using my mother's winning combination: fluffy basmati rice, sautéed greens and coconut sothi (page 232). It takes me right back to my childhood.

OKRA + TOMATO CURRY

Okra, also known as lady's fingers, is one of the most widely used vegetables in Sri Lanka and also famously used in Nigerian cuisine. It has become a favourite health food staple due to its high fibre content. Tomato pairs well with the earthy notes of okra in this colourful curry.

300g okra
1 tomato, diced
1 Tbsp olive oil
¾ tsp mustard seeds
¾ tsp cumin seeds
½ tsp ginger, minced
4 garlic cloves, sliced
1 onion, diced
a sprig curry leaves
1 green chilli, sliced
salt to taste
1 tsp curry powder (Jaffna style)*
½ tsp turmeric powder
¼ cup coriander leaves, chopped

*Refer to Spice Blends chapter

1. Wash and trim the okra and cut into 3cm pieces.
2. Heat the oil in a deep pan. Fry the mustard and cumin seeds.
3. When the seeds begin to sputter, add the ginger, garlic, onion, curry leaves and green chilli. Sauté for 2–3 minutes.
4. Add the okra pieces with salt and stir fry for 2–3 minutes.
5. Stir in the turmeric, curry powder, salt and diced tomatoes. Place a lid on the pan and cook for a further 5–6 minutes, stirring occasionally.
6. Stir in the coriander leaves and remove from the heat. Serve with hot rice or chapati.

SERVES 4
PREP 30 MINS
COOKING 30 MINS

 Given that this curry is only a little spicy, we recommend a Gruner Vetliner or a French Rosé.

SAMBAR

Sambar is a lentil-based vegetable stew prepared with tamarind, sambar powder and asafoetida. It has the consistency of a thick soup and is traditionally served as a side dish with rice, dosa or idli. This is a great way to get your daily serving of veges!

1 cup toor dal
a golf ball-sized piece of compressed tamarind
15g each of eggplant, carrots, beans, courgettes, okra, pumpkin, radish or any vegetables of your choice
3–4 cups of water
salt to taste
1 onion, cut into chunks
1 tsp turmeric powder
3 tsp chilli powder
2 tomatoes, quartered
2–3 Tbsp sambar powder*
1 Tbsp olive oil
2 tsp mustard seeds
2 tsp asafoetida powder
4 dried red chillies
2 sprigs of curry leaves
3 green chillies
½ tsp fenugreek seeds
½ cup chopped coriander leaves

*Refer to Spice Blends chapter

1. Soak the tamarind in water for 8–10 minutes. Extract the tamarind pulp and discard the membranes and seeds.

2. Wash and boil the dal with sufficient water until soft. Set aside.

3. Trim and peel the vegetables. Place in a saucepan, add 3–4 cups water, salt, onion, turmeric, chilli powder, tomatoes and cook until soft.

4. Add the cooked dal, tamarind pulp, and sambar powder. Boil for 10–15 minutes.

5. In a separate pan, heat the oil and fry the mustard seeds until they begin to sputter.

6. Add the asafoetida, dried chillies, curry leaves, green chillies and fenugreek seeds. Fry until lightly coloured.

7. Add this spicy mix to the vegetable mixture, boil for 1 minute and remove from the heat.

8. Stir in chopped coriander leaves. Serve with rice or dosa.

SERVES 4–6
PREP 30 MINS
COOKING 60 MINS

SNAKE BEAN CURRY

Snake beans are the most commonly used fresh bean variety in Sri Lanka. They are a good source of protein and an excellent curry option for vegetarians. This dish was created to bring out the best in the snake bean. Freshly squeezed lime juice adds a pleasant tartness to this simple curry.

425g snake beans
2–3 tsp oil
2 medium pink shallots, diced
1–2 green chillies
1 clove of garlic, finely chopped
1 small potato, cut into cubes
a sprig of curry leaves
1 tsp turmeric powder
½ tsp chilli powder
salt to taste
½ cup coconut milk
¼ cup water
¼ tsp fenugreek seeds
1 tsp roasted fennel powder*
juice of ½ a lime
*Refer to Spice Blends chapter

SERVES 4
PREP 30 MINS
COOKING 30 MINS

1 Cut the snake beans into 5cm pieces, wash and drain.

2 Heat the oil in a saucepan and sauté the shallots, chillies, garlic, potato cubes and curry leaves until fragrant. Stir in the fenugreek seeds.

3 Stir in the sliced beans, turmeric, chilli powder, salt, coconut milk and water. Cook for 6–8 minutes or until the liquid is absorbed. Stir the mixture occasionally. Do not overcook the beans. They should be bright green, tender and crisp.

4 Remove from the heat, sprinkle with roasted fennel powder and stir in the lime juice.

 Substitute the potato with cauliflower for a low-carb alternative.

POTATO MASALA

This Sri Lankan potato masala curry is one of our family favourites. I like to serve it with deep fried puri, chapati or crispy dosa. A simple but tasty recipe to have up your sleeve when you need a vegetarian curry in a hurry!

3 medium potatoes,
salt to taste
1 Tbsp vegetable oil
1 tsp mustard seeds
1 tsp cumin seeds
1 medium red onion, sliced
a sprig of curry leaves
2 long green chillies, sliced
1 tsp ginger, finely minced
4–6 cardamom pods
8cm cinnamon quill
2–3 cloves
½ tsp turmeric powder
1 tsp curry powder
¼ cup thick coconut milk
½ cup water
1 medium tomato, diced
juice of ¼–½ a lime
½ cup coriander leaves, chopped

SERVES 4
PREP 30 MINS
COOKING 45 MINS

1. Wash the potatoes and boil in salted water for 25–30 minutes or until cooked. Peel and cut into cubes and set aside.

2. Heat the oil in a large saucepan over a medium heat. Add the mustard and cumin seeds and fry until they start to sputter. Stir in the onion, curry leaves, chillies and ginger. Cook for 2–3 minutes until lightly coloured.

3. Remove the seeds from the cardamom pods. Place in a blender with cinnamon and cloves. Grind coarsely.

4. Add the ground spices, turmeric and curry powders to the onion mixture. Fry for few seconds until aromatic.

5. Add the potatoes, coconut milk, water, and diced tomato. Simmer with the lid on for 15–20 minutes, until the curry thickens. Stir occasionally to prevent the gravy sticking to the bottom of the pan.

6. Remove from the heat, mix in the lime juice, garnish with fresh coriander leaves and serve with hot Indian flat breads.

LENTIL CURRY W/ FRIED ONION GARNISH

Lentil curry (dal) is an important part of Sri Lankan cuisine and is eaten almost everywhere in the Indian subcontinent. This delicious lentil curry is infused with garlic and ground spices and garnished with fried onions, dried chillies and curry leaves. This curry ticks all the boxes for a nutritious, vegetarian dish.

2 cups red lentils
½ Tbsp oil
½ tsp mustard seeds
¼ tsp cumin seeds
1 medium onion, diced
2 green chillies
2 dried red chillies
a sprig of curry leaves
6 cloves of garlic
1 tsp turmeric powder
2–3 cups water
1 medium tomato, diced
1 cup fresh milk
salt to taste
2 tsp freshly ground cumin
1 tsp freshly ground black pepper

For the garnish
2 tsp oil
¼ tsp fennel seeds
¼ tsp mustard seeds
1 Tbsp sliced onion
a sprig of curry leaves
2 dried red chillies, cut into small pieces

1. Cover the lentils in water and soak for 10 minutes. Drain and rinse thoroughly.

2. Heat the oil in a saucepan and fry the mustard and cumin seeds. When the seeds begin to sputter, add the onion, chillies and the curry leaves. Crush 4 of the cloves of garlic and add them to the pan.

3. When the onion becomes translucent, add washed lentils, turmeric powder and 2–3 cups of water. Cook over a medium heat until the lentils are soft. Add more water if necessary.

4. Add the tomato, stir in the milk and cook for 6–8 minutes, or until the mixture thickens.

5. Crush the remaining 2 garlic cloves and add to the pan along with salt, ground cumin and black pepper. Stir well until combined. Remove from the heat.

For the garnish

6. Heat the oil in a frying pan and fry the fennel and mustard seeds for 30 seconds. Add the onion, curry leaves and dry chillies and fry for 2–3 minutes, or until golden and fragrant. Scatter over the dal curry before serving.

SERVES 4
PREP 30 MINS
COOKING 30 MINS

MY PARENTS AND ANCESTORS OBSERVED A MEAT-FREE REGIME A FEW DAYS A WEEK FOR CULTURAL AND RELIGIOUS REASONS. HENCE OUR TRADITIONAL ANCESTRAL MENU FEATURES AN ARRAY OF VEGETARIAN CURRY FEASTS.

FRIED EGGPLANT CURRY

This is a traditional vegetarian dish often served at weddings and special occasion banquets. Deep fried eggplant is cooked in a tamarind-based sauce and infused with a sensational Sri Lankan flavours.

350g eggplant
a golf ball-sized piece of compressed tamarind
½ cup water
oil for deep frying
1 Tbsp oil
1 large onion, sliced
6 cloves of garlic, peeled and sliced
2 green chillies, sliced
a sprig of curry leaves
¼ tsp fennel seeds
½ tsp fenugreek seeds
3 Tbsp curry powder (Jaffna style)*
1 cup coconut milk
salt to taste
*Refer to Spice Blends chapter

SERVES 4
PREP 30 MINS
COOKING 30 MINS

1. Place the tamarind in the water and set aside to soak for 8–10 minutes. Extract the tamarind pulp and discard the membranes and seeds.

2. Rinse and cut the eggplant into 6cm pieces.

3. Heat the oil in a large pan and deep fry the eggplant pieces. Drain and spread on three layers of paper towels.

4. In a separate pan, heat 1 Tbsp of oil and sauté the sliced onion, garlic, chillies and curry leaves until golden.

5. Add the fennel and fenugreek seeds and fry for 30 seconds until the mixture is aromatic.

6. Place the fried eggplant, onion mixture, curry powder, salt, tamarind pulp and coconut milk in a saucepan and bring to a boil. Reduce the heat and simmer for 10–12 minutes, or until the curry sauce thickens. Remove from the heat.

7. Serve with rice and curries, puttu or chapati.

TOMATO KULAMBU

This flavoursome tomato curry is my daughter's favourite vegetarian curry and is gloriously simple to make.

450g ripe tomatoes
1 Tbsp oil
1 tsp mustard seeds
¼ tsp cumin seeds
8cm piece pandan leaf
a sprig of curry leaves
1 large red onion, sliced
1 green chilli, sliced
6 garlic cloves, peeled and sliced into halves
2cm piece of ginger, minced
4 tsp curry powder (Jaffna style)*
½ tsp turmeric powder
¼ tsp fenugreek seeds
salt to taste
1–1½ cups water
1 cup coconut milk
a handful of coriander leaves for garnish
*Refer to Spice Blends chapter

SERVES 4
PREP 30 MINS
COOKING 30 MINS

1 Dice the tomatoes. If you prefer, blanch the tomatoes and remove the skin beforehand.

2 Heat the oil in a saucepan and fry the mustard and cumin seeds until the seeds begin to sputter. Stir in the pandan leaf, curry leaves, onion, chilli, garlic and ginger and sauté for 3–4 minutes until the onion is translucent and lightly golden.

3 Add the curry and turmeric powders and the fenugreek seeds to the onion mixture. Cook for 1 minute, until the spices are aromatic.

4 Combine the tomato pieces, salt, water and coconut milk with the onion mixture. Cover and gently simmer for 30–35 minutes, or until the sauce thickens. Garnish with coriander leaves before serving. Serve with rice and a lentil curry.

This can be adapted to an egg curry in a matter of minutes. Simply hard boil 4 or 5 eggs, peel, and make a few shallow cuts. Add the eggs to the prepared tomato gravy.

RASAM

Rasam is a thin, spicy South Indian broth traditionally made with tamarind, coriander, cumin, black pepper and loads of garlic. Nature's amazing ingredients in this stock give a soothing and healing effect. Quite often, I serve this as an appetiser and my guests refer it to as "liquid gold from Sai's kitchen".

For the rasam spice
- 1 Tbsp coriander seeds
- ½ Tbsp cumin seeds
- ¼ Tbsp black peppercorns

For the broth
- a small golf ball-sized piece of compressed tamarind
- 4 cups water
- 1 medium ripened tomato, diced
- 1 green chilli, slit in half
- salt to taste
- 1 tsp mustard seeds
- ¼ Tbsp cumin seeds
- a raisin-sized piece of asafoetida
- 2-3 dried chillies
- 6-8 cloves of garlic, crushed
- 1 sprig of curry leaves
- ¼ cup coriander leaves

SERVES 4
PREP 30 MINS
COOKING 30 MINS

To make the rasam spice mixture
1. Place the coriander, cumin seeds and black pepper in a mortar and coarsely grind. Cover and set aside until required.

To make the broth
2. Soak the tamarind in the water for 6-8 minutes. Squeeze and extract the tamarind juice, strain and discard the membranes and seeds.

3. Transfer the tamarind juice to a saucepan. Add salt and diced tomato, and bring to a boil.

4. In a separate pan, heat the oil and fry the mustard and cumin seeds. When the mustard begins to pop, add the asafoetida and fry for 10 seconds. Add the dried chillies, crushed garlic, curry leaves and ground rasam spice, and fry for 25-35 seconds until aromatic. Add this spice mix to the tamarind broth.

5. When the tamarind mixture starts to boil rapidly, add the coriander leaves and green chilli. Continue to cook for a further 25-30 seconds. Remove from the heat and serve.

ATCHARU/MIXED PICKLE, PAGE 283.

SAMBAL
+PICKLES
+CHUTNEYS

HOMEMADE PICKLES AND CHUTNEYS ADD ZING AND EXCITEMENT TO ANY MEAL. TRY THESE WITH CURRIES, ROASTS, IN SANDWICHES OR WITH CHEESE AND CRACKERS.

COCONUT SAMBAL, PAGE 272.

SWEET MANGO CHUTNEY

My mother used to make the most wonderful chutney with mangoes freshly picked from her garden in Sri Lanka. A touch of sweetness complements piquant curry dishes or grilled meats and seafood. Delicious to serve with cheese and crackers, this mango chutney can also be added to marinades to help develop flavour.

450g fresh green mangoes
8–10 cardamom pods
8 black peppercorns
½ tsp mustard seeds
8cm cinnamon stick
6 whole cloves
2 tsp dried red chilli, crushed
1 tsp Kashmiri chilli powder
3cm piece fresh ginger
3 cloves of garlic
350g white sugar
1 cup white vinegar
½ cup water
salt to taste

MAKES 700–750G
PREP 30 MINS
COOKING 60 MINS

1. Wash and peel the mangoes. Cut into 3cm pieces.

2. Remove the cardamom seeds from their pods. Put into a grinder with the black peppercorns, mustard, cinnamon, cloves and chilli and grind to a powder. Process with the ginger and garlic to make a coarse paste.

4. In a non-stick saucepan, place the diced mango, sugar, vinegar, water and salt. Bring to a boil. Cover and cook over a medium heat for 15 minutes. Stir occasionally to prevent the mixture sticking to the bottom of the pan.

5. Stir in the spice paste and continue to cook on a low heat for 45–50 minutes, or until the mixture reaches jam-like consistency.

6. Store in sterilised jars and refrigerate once opened.

 Try this recipe using fresh quince instead of mango. It works superbly!

COCONUT SAMBAL

Sri Lankan coconut sambal is popular around the globe. Sambal was traditionally made using a rectangular grinding stone with a roller. Nowadays, it takes only a few minutes to prepare in a food processor.

2 cups freshly grated coconut
10–12 dried red chillies
1–2 small pink shallots
15–18 curry leaves
salt to taste
juice of ½ a lime

SERVES 4
PREP 30 MINS

1. Place the chillies in a food processor and crush into a coarse powder.

2. Add the grated coconut, pink shallots and curry leaves, and grind to a coarse mixture.

3. Add the salt and fresh lime juice. Mix well.

4. Serve as a relish with hoppers, chapati, naan, pittu or string hoppers. It tastes delicious with just about anything!

If freshly grated coconut is unavailable, use frozen grated coconut, or desiccated coconut soaked in milk for a few minutes. For an exciting variation, add 2 tsps of Maldive fish chips to the prepared coconut sambal.

APPLE + CHILLI CHUTNEY

This sweet and sour chutney is hugely versatile. It makes a stunning accompaniment to rice and curries but is as good served with warm, buttered bread or in burgers and wraps. A spoonful of this chutney works like magic in marinades.

450g Granny Smith apples
10 green chillies, sliced
½ Tbsp white mustard seeds
½ Tbsp black mustard seeds
½ Tbsp black pepper
6cm piece ginger, finely minced
6 cloves of garlic, finely minced
8 cloves
12cm cinnamon stick
salt to taste
1 cup sugar
½ cup golden syrup

MAKES 400–500G
PREP 30 MINS
COOKING 90 MINS

1. Wash and dry the apples. Peel, core and cut them into wedges.

2. Place the mustard seeds and black pepper in a spice grinder and process into a coarse powder.

3. Place all the ingredients in a saucepan, cover and bring to a boil. After 15 minutes of rapid boiling, reduce the heat and let simmer.

4. It takes about 1–1½ hours for the chutney to thicken and correctly set. Stir occasionally to prevent the mixture catching on the bottom of the pan.

5. Remove from the heat and let cool in the pan. Store in sterilised jars.

BRINJAL/EGGPLANT PICKLE, PAGE 280.

BRINJAL/EGGPLANT PICKLE

Eggplant, known as brinjal, is commonly used in Sri Lankan cuisine. This pickle is an ideal companion for rice and meat curries or even with grilled meats, sandwiches and wraps.

200–250g eggplant
2 large red onions
4–5 green chillies
4cm piece ginger
6 garlic cloves
1 tsp mustard seeds
2 dried red chillies
oil for deep frying
¾ cup white vinegar
salt to taste
2–3 tsp sugar

SERVES 4–6
PREP 30 MINS
COOKING 60 MINS

1. Slice the onions and green chillies.

2. Cut the eggplant into 4cm pieces. Rub with salt and set aside in a colander for 15 minutes. Squeeze to remove the excess water. Spread on a tray lined with paper towels.

3. In a food processor, grind the ginger, garlic, mustard seeds and dried chillies to a coarse paste.

4. Heat oil in a frying pan and deep fry the eggplants in batches until golden brown. Drain and spread on two layers of paper towels.

5. Fry the onions and chillies until lightly golden, drain and spread on paper towels.

6. Place the spice paste, vinegar, sugar, salt, fried eggplants, onions and chillies in a clay pot or non-metallic pan. Bring to a boil for 1–2 minutes and remove from the heat. Set aside to cool.

7. Transfer to a sterilised jar. This pickle can be stored in the refrigerator for several weeks.

SPICY GUACAMOLE

The rich, buttery taste of guacamole delivers a luxurious finish to my seafood starters and it is sure to take your ordinary chips and dips to another level.

2 medium avocados
1 small ripe tomato, diced
1 green chilli, finely chopped
1 red chilli, finely chopped
1 small pink shallot, finely chopped
1 spring onion, finely chopped
½ cup coriander leaves, chopped
zest of ½ a lime
juice of one lime
salt and pepper to taste

SERVES 2–4
PREP 30 MINS

1 Cut the avocados in half and gently twist to remove the seeds.

2 Take a small knife and make cuts in the flesh in a criss-cross pattern. Take care not to break through the avocado skin.

3 Use a spoon to scoop out the avocado pieces into a clean bowl.

4 Add the rest of the ingredients and stir lightly to combine. Refrigerate until needed.

ATCHARU / MIXED PICKLE

Crunchy, sweet and tangy, atcharu is an indispensable item in most Sri Lankan households. A slight variation on my mum's basic recipe, I added dates for sweetness. It has enough punch to cut through the richness of meaty dishes.

175g carrot
125g green beans
100g shallots
100g dates
6–8 green chillies
2½ Tbsp mustard seeds
3–4 cloves garlic
1 Tbsp chilli flakes
½ cup white vinegar
1 Tbsp sugar
4cm piece ginger
salt to taste

SERVES 6–8
PREP 30 MINS
COOKING 30 MINS

1 Grind the mustard, garlic, chilli flakes, ginger and dates to a paste.

2 Mix the ground paste with 1 Tbsp of the vinegar and the sugar. Set aside.

3 Wash and pat dry the chillies, carrots and beans. Trim the carrots and beans and cut into 8cm-long pieces.

4 Trim, peel and wash the shallots. Dry with a paper towel.

5 Split the chillies in half lengthwise.

6 In a saucepan, bring to a boil the remaining vinegar with the salt. Add the vegetables and shallots and cook for 1–2 minutes. Remove from the heat.

7 Add the spice paste to the vegetable mixture and toss to coat evenly.

8 Cool and transfer to a sterilised jar. Store for at least 5–8 days for the flavours to fully develop.

Try using assorted seasonal chilli varieties for different tastes and textures.

TOMATO CHUTNEY

This silky smooth, low-calorie chutney is really versatile. It works well as an accompaniment, as a spread or a colourful dip. It is one of my favourite chutneys and I make it often in summer when fresh tomatoes are plentiful.

1½ cups ripe tomatoes, diced
2 tsp oil
1 tsp mustard seeds
1 tsp cumin seeds
3–4 dried red chillies
a sprig of curry leaves
5cm piece ginger
1 Tbsp chana dal
1 large red onion, peeled and diced
salt to taste

For the garnish
1 tsp oil
1 tsp mustard seeds
½ tsp cumin seeds
1 Tbsp chana dal
¾ tsp urad dal
a sprig of curry leaves

SERVES 4–6
PREP 30 MINS
COOKING 30 MINS

1. Heat the oil in a pan and fry the mustard and cumin seeds. As the seeds begin to sputter, add the dried chillies, curry leaves, chana dal and ginger and cook for 2–3 minutes.

2. Add the diced onion and sauté until translucent and fragrant.

3. Stir in the tomatoes and salt. Cook for a further 6–8 minutes until the onion and tomatoes soften. Remove from the heat.

4. Transfer the contents of the pan to a food processor and blend until smooth.

To make the garnish
5. Heat the oil in a separate pan and fry the mustard seeds. As they begin to sputter, add the rest of the ingredients and cook for 3–4 minutes until the mixture is golden and fragrant. Sprinkle over the chutney and serve.

SWEET TREATS

DESSERT IS THE FIRST THOUGHT THAT CROSSES MY MIND WHEN I AM PLANNING A BIG MEAL.

INDULGE YOUR
SWEET TOOTH WITH
THIS SUMPTUOUS
ARRAY OF DESSERTS.

MY GRANDDAUGHTER IS MY SOUS CHEF AND CRITIC WHEN IT COMES TO DESSERTS.

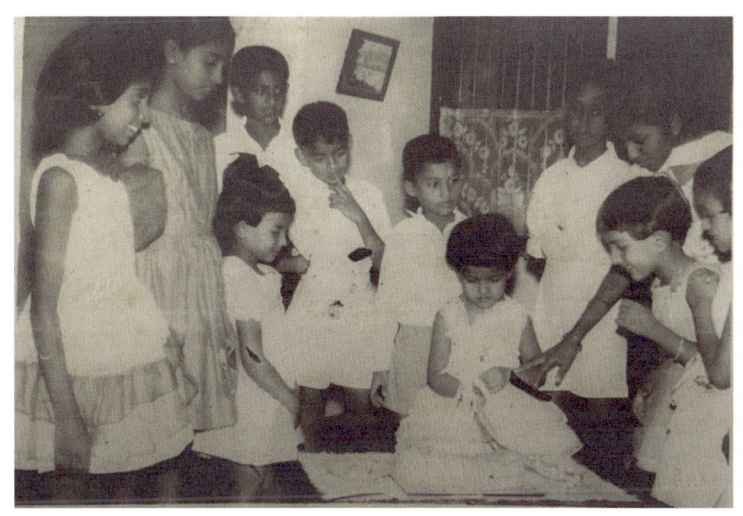

I'VE ALWAYS HAD A SWEET TOOTH!

ESPRESSO + WHITE CHOCOLATE MOUSSE W/ NUTTY COFFEE FINGERS

Thanks to my son and daughter-in-law for their gift of a capsule coffee machine, which prompted me to design this treat. Lusciously layered mousse paired with a crunchy coffee finger is the ultimate pudding for those coffee lovers out there.

25ml espresso (machine coffee, cooled)
200g white chocolate buttons
1 vanilla pod
2 gelatine leaves
300ml fresh cream
2 eggs, separated
2 tsp sugar
3 tsp good quality instant coffee

For the coffee fingers
100g butter
110g caster sugar
1 egg
1 tsp pure vanilla extract
60g ground almond
75g self-raising flour
¼ cup toasted hazelnuts, roughly chopped
1 x contents of espresso coffee capsule or 8g of freshly ground espresso coffee
¼ cup slivered almonds
1 Tbsp fresh cream

SERVES 6–8
PREP 60 MINS
+ SETTING
COOKING 30 MINS

To make the white chocolate mousse

1. Split the vanilla pod, scrape out the seeds with the edge of a sharp knife and transfer to a bowl with the white chocolate. Gently melt the chocolate in a bowl, over a saucepan of simmering water.

2. Soak the gelatine in cold water for 5–6 minutes. Squeeze to remove excess water. Mix with the melted chocolate until the gelatine dissolves. Remove from the heat. Don't panic if it looks thick and gluey at this stage. It will all come together nicely! Set aside.

3. Beat the egg yolks with the sugar until pale and creamy. Combine with the chocolate mixture.

4. Pour the cream into a bowl and whip until soft peaks form and it doubles in quantity. Be careful not to overwhip the cream. Gradually combine the chocolate and the whipped cream.

5. Whisk the egg whites in a separate bowl to stiff peaks. Gently fold into the chocolate mixture. Reserve 250ml of this mixture in a separate bowl for the top layer. Cover and set aside.

To make the base layer

6. Mix the instant coffee with the cooled espresso to intensify the flavours. Gradually combine this coffee with the chocolate cream mixture, one spoon at a time, making sure not to overmix. Fill serving cups with this this espresso mousse mixture. Refrigerate for 1 hour, or until set firm.

7. Take the white chocolate mousse you set aside earlier and spoon over the espresso layer. Refrigerate for 6–8 hours.

To make the coffee fingers

8 Preheat the oven to 180°C.

9 Cream the butter and sugar until light and fluffy. Beat the egg with the vanilla extract. Fold in the flour, ground almonds, hazelnuts and espresso coffee granules. Stir well to combine.

10 Line a 20cm x 30cm baking tray with baking paper. Spread this mixture evenly (about 2cm thick), scatter over the slivered almonds and press firmly with a spatula.

11 Bake for 30–35 minutes, or until golden and firm. Remove from the oven. While still warm, cut the biscuit into 2.5 x 8cm long fingers. Set aside to cool.

12 Serve the mousse in cups with coffee fingers on the side.

Try this with a Cream Sherry – it will complement the acidity of the coffee.

BANANA GINGER CAKE

Deliciously light and moist with a crunchy oat base, you will enjoy making this cake time after time.

For the cake
2 cups mashed bananas
125g plain flour plus extra for dusting
130g brown spelt flour
1 tsp ground cinnamon
2 tsp ground ginger
1 tsp baking powder
1 tsp baking soda
125g butter, softened plus extra for greasing
175g soft brown sugar
2 tsp vanilla extract
2 eggs
4 Tbsp golden syrup

For the oat crunch base
½ cup wholegrain oats
1 Tbsp golden syrup
2 Tbsp brown sugar
1 Tbsp butter
1 tsp ground ginger

SERVES 6–8
PREP 60 MINS
COOKING 60 MINS

1. Preheat the oven to 180°C.

2. Lightly grease a loaf tin (28cm x 10cm x 8cm) or mini loaf pans, dust with flour and shake off the excess.

To make the oat crunch base
3. Place all the ingredients in a bowl and stir gently to combine. Spoon this mixture into the greased cake tin or the mini loaf pans and spread.

To make the cake
4. Sift the flours, ginger, cinnamon, baking powder, and baking soda into a bowl.

5. In a separate bowl, place the butter, sugar and vanilla extract. Beat until pale and fluffy.

6. Add the eggs one at a time and beat until the mixture becomes light and creamy.

7. Fold in the mashed banana, mixed dry ingredients and golden syrup. Stir to combine.

8. Spoon the mixture over the oat crunch base and bake for 45–55 minutes. A skewer inserted into the centre should come out clean.

9. Remove the cake from the oven and cool in the tin for 20 minutes. Transfer to a wire rack to cool completely. Slice and serve.

V

LOVE CAKE

Love Cake is the preferred cake when it comes to our family celebrations. Adapted slightly from our family recipe, my version is laced with warming aromas and citrusy notes. This cake is sure to add a little Sri Lankan charm (and love) to any occasion.

150g softened butter
300g caster sugar
4 whole eggs plus 2 extra yolks
zest of 1 orange
zest of 1 lemon
1 tsp honey
2 Tbsp pure rose water
1 tsp grated nutmeg
2 tsp vanilla extract
2 tsp mixed allspice powder*
150g cashew nuts, ground
150g semolina, roasted
150g pumpkin preserve
½ cup pistachios, roughly chopped
2 Tbsp pistachios, finely chopped for garnish
*Refer to Spice Blends chapter

1 Preheat the oven to 175°C. Line a cake tin (23cm x 23cm x 3.5cm) with a layer of foil. Place a layer of baking paper over the foil.

2 Cream the sugar and butter until light and fluffy. Add the eggs and egg yolks one at a time, beating well after each addition.

3 Add the orange and lemon zests, honey, rose water, vanilla, nutmeg, allspice powder, ground cashews, semolina, roughly chopped pistachios and pumpkin preserve. Gently fold to combine.

4 Pour the mixture into the cake tin and bake for 30–45 minutes or until lightly golden on top. Insert a skewer into the centre of the cake and it should come out clean with no traces of cake batter.

5 Remove from the oven and allow to cool completely. Scatter over the remaining chopped pistachios. For complete decadence, serve with warm orange syrup.

SERVES 12–15
PREP 60 MINS
COOKING 45 MINS

Pumpkin preserve is available at most Sri Lankan grocers. If unavailable, replace it with crystallised ginger. Due to its high sugar content, Love Cake has the tendency to brown very quickly. Keep a close watch while baking. If necessary, cover loosely with tin foil.

MUM'S SIGNATURE BUTTER CAKE

A deliciously moist butter cake recipe which my whole family loves – and yes, the vanilla measurement in this recipe is correct!

500g butter
500g caster sugar
8 large eggs, separated
500g high grade flour
4 tsp baking powder
2 Tbsp vanilla extract
½ cup milk
⅛ tsp freshly grated nutmeg

For the topping
½ cup sliced or slivered almonds
a handful of cashew nuts, chopped
½ cup raisins

SERVES 10–12
PREP 30 MINS
COOKING 60 MINS

1 Preheat the oven to 180°C.

2 Grease a cake tin (40cm x 32cm x 8cm) and line with baking paper.

3 Cream the butter and sugar until pale and fluffy. Add the egg yolks one by one, beating well after each addition.

3 In a separate bowl, beat the egg whites with a pinch of salt to soft peak stage.

4 Sift the flour and baking powder into a bowl. Gradually fold the flour and egg whites into the butter mixture. Be careful not to overmix.

5 Add the vanilla extract, milk and grated nutmeg and stir to combine. Pour the batter into the prepared tin. Top evenly with nuts and raisins. Tap the sides of the cake tin and place the cake in the oven.

6 Bake for 45–55 minutes, or until an inserted skewer comes out clean. Remove the cake from the oven and cool in the tin for 20 minutes. Transfer to a wire rack to cool completely. Slice and serve.

 This lovely cake is the perfect accompaniment to a cup of tea and equally good to serve as a dessert with fresh blueberries and a scoop of vanilla ice cream.

MUM'S DELICIOUS DATE CAKE, PAGE 305.

CHOC-NUT BROWNIES W/ CHANTILLY CREAM

These brownies are easy to create and delightful to eat! Balanced flavours from fine quality chocolate produce a moist slice with an excellent texture. Fabulous served with Chantilly cream but these choc-nut brownies also taste delicious on their own.

300g full-bodied dark chocolate (e.g. 70% Cocoa)
¼ cup lightly toasted hazelnuts, chopped roughly
¼ cup slivered almonds, lightly toasted
150g butter, cubed
250g soft brown sugar
4 eggs, lightly beaten
150g plain flour
125ml fresh cream
1 tsp pure vanilla extract

For garnish
cocoa powder
icing sugar for dusting

For Chantilly cream
200ml thickened cream
3 tsp icing sugar
1 tsp pure vanilla extract with seeds

MAKES 20
PREP 30 MINS
COOKING 30 MINS

1. Preheat oven to 180°C. Grease a baking pan (20cm x 30cm), and line with baking paper.

2. Place butter and chocolate in a heatproof bowl over a saucepan of simmering water. Make sure the water doesn't touch the bottom of the bowl and that the chocolate doesn't come into contact with the water or steam. When the melted chocolate mixture is glossy, remove from the heat and set aside.

3. In a bowl, beat the sugar and eggs until pale. Mix in the flour, nuts, vanilla, cream and the melted chocolate mixture. Do not overwork this mixture!

4. Pour into the lined baking pan and bake for 25–30 minutes.

5. Remove from the oven and let the brownie cool in the pan. Cut into squares and dust lightly with cocoa powder or icing sugar or a combination of both.

6. To make Chantilly cream, whisk all the ingredients together until soft peaks form. Serve on the side of the brownies.

If you are making this for vegatarians, be aware that some thickened cream contains gelatine. Be sure to look for a brand that uses vegetable gums as a thickening agent. Alternatively, use fresh cream.

MUM'S DELICIOUS DATE CAKE

This beautifully moist date cake studded with crunchy nuts is another recipe I inherited from my mother. This cake has a caramelised top layer and keeps well – in fact it seems to get better tasting by the day! This is a perfect indulgent treat to enjoy with a cup of freshly brewed Ceylon tea.

1kg seedless dates
1½ cups warm water
2 tsp baking soda
450g golden caster sugar or light brown sugar
8 large eggs
450g cake flour
360g butter
3 tsp baking powder
2 Tbsp vanilla extract
130g cashew nuts, coarsely ground
¾ cup almonds, sliced

SERVES 12–15
PREP 30 MINS
+ SOAKING
COOKING 60 MINS

1 Chop the dates into small pieces and transfer to a large bowl. Mix the baking soda with warm water and pour over the chopped dates. Mix well, cover and set aside overnight.

2 Line a cake tin (38cm x 27cm x 7.5cm) with two layers of foil. Place a layer of baking paper over the foil. Preheat the oven to 180°C.

3 Cream the butter and sugar until creamy and light. Add the eggs, beating well after each addition.

4 Sift the flour and baking powder together and gradually incorporate into the butter mixture.

5 Add the date mixture and the ground cashew nuts and fold in. Add vanilla and gently combine, taking care not to overmix.

6 Transfer the cake batter into the prepared tin. Scatter evenly with sliced almonds. Tap the sides of the cake tin and bake for 45–50 minutes.

7 Test by inserting a skewer into the centre of the cake. It should come out clean with no traces of cake batter.

8 Remove from the oven and cool in the tin for 30 minutes. Remove from the tin and transfer to a wire cake rack to cool completely.

Start this well ahead of time, as the dates are best soaked overnight. Once in the oven, the cake will start to brown very quickly so keep a close watch. If it looks like it is browning too quickly, cover it with foil.

RASPBERRY FRANGIPANE TARTLETS

These divine tartlets are packed with moist almond filling and encased in a buttery golden pastry, beautifully studded with luscious raspberries. A vibrant berry compote adds extra freshness to the dish.

8 blind-baked, mini pastry cases, left in baking tin*

For the frangipane filling
250g butter, softened
250g caster sugar
5 eggs
300g ground almonds
40g plain flour
1½ tsp pure vanilla extract
½ tsp almond extract
½ tsp pure rose water
zest of ½ a lemon
2 punnets of raspberries (400–500g)

For the raspberry compote
2 Tbsp water
2 cups raspberries
110g sugar
zest of ½ a lemon
1 tsp vanilla extract

*Refer to page 54

SERVES 10–12
PREP 30 MINS
COOKING 60 MINS

To make the frangipane filling
1. Cream the butter and sugar in a bowl. Add the eggs one by one.

2. Fold in the ground almonds, flour, vanilla, almond extract, rose water and lemon zest.

3. Spoon this mixture into the pastry cases and arrange raspberries on top. Bake for 15–20 minutes, or until lightly golden. Cool in the tin before removing.

To make the compote
4. Place all the ingredients except the vanilla in a saucepan and bring to a boil. Lower the heat and leave to simmer for approximately 8 minutes. Remove from the heat, add the vanilla extract and let cool.

To serve
5. Serve the tartlets with vanilla bean ice cream, extra raspberries and berry compote on the side.

Store any excess raspberry compote in a clean jar. It can be kept for up to a week in the fridge. It tastes great with plain vanilla or chocolate ice cream when you want a simple sweet treat. Try it on pancakes for an indulgent brunch!

LOVE CAKE TARTLETS W/ GINGER + CITRUS

The Sri Lankan Love Cake is reinvented into a fancy dessert with ginger and citrusy notes. Orange segments and sorbet add depth, and balance the sweet richness of the cake.

8 blind-baked, mini pastry cases*

For the orange sorbet
1 litre fresh orange juice
¼ tsp orange blossom extract
3 Tbsp caster sugar

For the Love Cake filling
75g softened butter
125g caster sugar
2 whole eggs plus 1 extra yolk
zest of ½ an orange
zest of ½ a lemon
½ tsp honey
1 Tbsp pure rose water
1 tsp vanilla extract
½ tsp grated nutmeg
1 tsp mixed allspice powder**
75g ground cashew nuts
75g semolina, roasted
75g crystallised ginger, finely chopped
¼ cup pistachios, roughly chopped

To serve
2 oranges, cut into segments
mint leaves
ground pistachios
*Refer to page 54
**Refer to Spice Blends chapter

SERVES 8
PREP 60 MINS
COOKING 30 MINS

To make the sorbet
1. Mix together the orange juice, orange blossom extract and caster sugar until dissolved. Churn in an ice cream maker and store in a freezer-proof container and freeze until required.

To make the filling
2. Cream the butter and sugar until light and fluffy. Add the eggs and extra yolk one at a time, beating well after each addition.

3. Add the citrus zests, honey, rose water, vanilla, nutmeg, allspice powder, ground cashews, semolina, and crystallised ginger and fold lightly until combined.

To make the tartlets
4. Preheat the oven to 175°C. Arrange the pastry cases on a baking tray and fill each tartlet with Love Cake mixture. Sprinkle with coarsely chopped pistachios and bake for 30 minutes until the filling is golden and cooked.

5. Remove from the oven and allow to cool.

6. Serve with the orange segments, sorbet, mint and a dusting of ground pistachios.

If you don't have an ice cream maker, freeze the sorbet mixture in ice cube trays for a few hours. Blend the ice cubes in a blender and return to the freezer until ready to serve. Due to its high sugar content, Love Cake has the tendency to brown very quickly. Keep a close watch and cover with foil if necessary.

ORANGE-INFUSED CRÈME CARAMEL

Caramel pudding is an all-time favourite for most Sri Lankans. During a trip to Spain, I discovered that caramel custard is also the most popular dessert there. After experimenting with different ingredients, I reinvented this decadent orange and vanilla infused crème caramel. This classic dessert gets a citrusy lift and is sure to impress anyone.

220g caster sugar plus 55g extra
butter for greasing
125ml water
625ml full cream milk
300ml fresh cream
4 eggs, plus 2 egg yolks
zest of two oranges
2 tsp vanilla bean paste or pure vanilla extract

SERVES 6–8
PREP 60 MINS + CHILLING
COOKING 45 MINS

1. Preheat oven to 180°C. Grease six individual ramekins or a 20cm round baking dish with butter.

2. Place 220g sugar and water in a saucepan and heat over a medium heat. Stir until the sugar dissolves and bring it to a boil. Cook for 10–12 minutes until the mixture reaches a dark golden colour. Keep a close watch as the sugar syrup will begin to colour very quickly.

3. Pour the caramel syrup into the greased ramekins or the baking dish and allow the caramel to set.

4. In the same saucepan, combine milk, cream, orange zest and vanilla bean paste and bring to a boil. Remove from the heat and stand for 15 minutes.

5. In a bowl, whisk the whole eggs, yolks, and the remaining sugar. Add the warm milk mixture and beat to combine. Strain into a jug and pour over the caramel.

6. Lay a paper towel on the bottom of a large roasting tray and arrange the ramekins or baking dish. Carefully pour hot water into the tray, to come halfway up the sides of the ramekins or dish.

To ensure the caramel is properly dissolved and you get the perfect syrupy finish, I recommend starting this dessert a day ahead. I serve this dish with vanilla ice cream and my ginger macadamia wafers, page 325.

7 Place the tray in the oven and bake for 35 minutes, or until cooked. When shaken, it should be wobbly!

8 Remove from the oven and let cool. Refrigerate for 24 hours.

9 Run a small spatula around the edges of the ramekins or baking dish Release the crème caramel and turn onto a serving plate.

RASPBERRY CRÈME BRÛLÉE

I designed this fruity twist on the French classic by adding poached berries. Golden caramelised walnut nuggets and bright fresh raspberries on the side finish this elegant dessert.

For raspberry crème brûlée
2 x 250ml fresh cream
1 vanilla pod, split
5 large egg yolks
50g caster sugar
110g caster sugar for burnt sugar layer

For the caramelised walnuts
½ cup shelled walnuts, roughly chopped
1 tsp butter
55g caster sugar
1 Tbsp water

For the poached raspberries
18–24 plump fresh raspberries
50g caster sugar
50ml water
½ a vanilla pod, split

For garnish
fresh raspberries
mint leaves

SERVES 6–8
PREP 30 MINS + CHILLING
COOKING 60 MINS

To make the caramelised walnuts
1. Lightly toast the nuts with the butter in a frying pan. In a saucepan, cook the sugar and water over a high heat for 7–8 minutes until the sugar begins to caramelise. Stir in the toasted walnuts and mix well to coat. Spread the mixture evenly on a tray lined with baking paper. Once cool, break into bite-sized nuggets. Set aside.

To make the poached raspberries
2. Bring the sugar, water and vanilla to a boil. As the syrup begins to bubble, remove from the heat, add the raspberries and set aside to cool.

To make the crème brûlée
3. Preheat the oven to 180–200°C.

4. In a bowl, whisk the egg yolks until pale and thick.

5. Cut the vanilla pod lengthwise with a sharp knife. Split it in two and scrape out all the seeds. Place the vanilla pod, seeds and cream in a saucepan.

6. Heat the cream and vanilla over a medium heat. Bring to the boil and when bubbles start to appear around the edge, remove from the heat.

7. Gradually pour the hot cream into the beaten egg mixture, stirring constantly with a whisk. Strain this cream mixture through a fine sieve over a large bowl. Make sure to scrape through all of the vanilla seeds. Carefully skim off the froth with a spoon and discard.

8 Prepare a water bath by placing a single layer of paper towels inside a roasting tray and arrange 6–8 ramekins inside. Place three poached raspberries in each ramekin. Carefully pour in the hot cream mixture, filling the ramekins right to the top. Pour hot water into the roasting tray until roughly halfway up the sides of the ramekins.

9 Carefully transfer the tray to the oven. Place a sheet of baking paper over the top of the ramekins to cover. This step is optional but it helps to prevent the formation of a skin on the custard.

10 Bake for 25–30 minutes or until the mixture is softly set. To test, gently shake a ramekin. The custard should still be wobbly in the middle.

11 Lift the ramekins out of the roasting tray and allow to cool before refrigerating overnight.

12 Sprinkle 1½ tsp of caster sugar over each brûlée and spread evenly with the back of a spoon, completely covering the surface.

13 Use a cook's blow torch and hold the flame just above the sugar. Continuously move the blow torch until the sugar caramelises. Let the dessert stand for a few minutes allowing the sugar to form a crust. Serve with raspberries and walnut nuggets. Garnish with mint leaves.

It is best to prepare this dish well ahead of time, preferably the day before you plan to serve it. Prepare the custard and leave it in the fridge overnight, then complete the last step of creating the burnt sugar crust just before serving.

MUM'S SIGNATURE BUTTER CAKE, PAGE 300.

MANGO PUDDING W/ CARAMEL PISTACHIOS + SAGO PEARLS

Mango, a sweet-scented tropical indulgence. Growing up, I was lucky enough to be able to pick mangoes right from my backyard. This delightful dessert is my tribute to Jaffna mangoes. Salted caramel pistachios lend texture to the ripe, fragrant fruit. There's no better time than summer to make this refreshing pudding.

1 ripe mango, diced and puréed (300ml of mango pulp)
1 ripe mango for garnish
2 gelatine leaves
45ml condensed milk
45g sugar
4 egg yolks
350ml regular milk
180ml fresh cream
2 tsp pure vanilla extract

For the salted-caramel pistachios
85g shelled pistachios
110g caster sugar
¼ tsp sea salt
60ml water

For the sago pearls
1 Tbsp sago
250ml water

SERVES 6–8
PREP 45 MINS
+ CHILLING
COOKING 30 MINS

To make the pudding

1 Soak the gelatine leaves in cold water.

2 In a large bowl, whisk the condensed milk with sugar and egg yolks until the mixture becomes pale and thick.

3 Bring the regular milk to a boil in a saucepan. Add this hot milk to the egg mixture, whisking steadily.

4 Squeeze out the water from the soaked gelatine. Add the gelatine leaves to the bowl. Stir until dissolved. Add the vanilla extract and set aside to cool. Gradually incorporate the mango purée into the milk and gelatine combination.

5 In a separate bowl, whisk the cream to soft peaks. Fold into the mango mixture. Pour into serving dishes or goblets and allow to set in the refrigerator for 4–5 hours.

To make the salted caramel pistachios

6 Place the sugar, sea salt and water in a saucepan and cook over a high heat for 7–8 minutes. As the syrup begins to caramelise, stir in the pistachios and mix well to coat. Spread the mixture on a tray lined with baking paper. Once cool, break into small pieces. Set aside until required.

To make the sago pearls

7 Place the water in a small saucepan and bring it to a boil. Add the sago and boil for 5–6 minutes until the pearls are translucent. Remove from the heat and transfer into a strainer. Rinse well under running water.

To serve

8 Peel and dice the extra mango. Decorate the pudding with diced mango, sago pearls and sea-salted caramel pistachios.

CARDAMOM PANNA COTTA W/ RASPBERRY ROSE JELLY + SPICED BISCUITS

The unusual flavour combination of cardamom, raspberry and rose produce a harmonious outcome in this glorious summer dessert. Serve with the cardamom-spiced biscuit and delight your guests.

For the raspberry rose jelly
1 cup raspberries
4 Tbsp caster sugar
250ml water
¾ tsp powdered gelatine
1 tsp pure rose water

For the panna cotta
600ml light fresh cream
4 Tbsp caster sugar
2 tsp powdered gelatine
2 tsp cardamom pods, crushed
1–2 tsp pure rose water

For the spiced biscuits
100g butter
100g caster sugar
1 egg white
100g flour
1½ tsp cardamom seeds, freshly ground
70g ground almonds
¼ tsp almond extract
2–3 Tbsp pistachios, roughly chopped

For the garnish
dried roses
fresh raspberries

SERVES 4
PREP 60 MINS
+ SETTING
COOKING 30 MINS

To make the jelly
1. Place the water, raspberry and sugar in a saucepan and bring to a boil. Cook for 2–3 minutes, remove from the heat and sprinkle on the powdered gelatine. Add the rose water and stir until the gelatine dissolves. Pass through a strainer and set aside to cool.

2. Oil 4 panna cotta moulds and wipe off excess oil with a clean tissue. Divide the jelly equally among the moulds. Refrigerate until it sets firm.

To make the panna cotta
3. Place the cream, sugar, gelatine and cardamom in a small saucepan over low heat. Cook without boiling, until sugar and gelatine dissolve. Remove from the heat and add the rose water. Set aside to cool and allow the flavours to infuse.

4. Strain through a sieve into a jug and pour over the set jelly. Refrigerate for several hours or overnight.

To make the biscuits
5. Preheat the oven to 180°C. Place the butter and sugar in a bowl and beat until creamy and light. Add the egg white and continue to beat the mixture until creamy. Fold in the flour, ground cardamom, ground almonds and almond extract until combined.

6. Line a baking tray (20cm x 30cm) with baking paper and place the biscuit mixture on top. Spread out the mixture thinly and evenly with a spatula. Sprinkle the pistachios on top and bake in the oven for 20–22 minutes or until golden. Remove from the oven and cut into desired shape while still warm.

To serve

7 Garnish the panna cotta and jelly with dried roses and fresh raspberries. Serve with the spiced biscuits and raspberry coulis.

Pair this dessert with a medium-sweet Gewurztraminer. Moscato D'Asti and Asti Spumante have nice floral notes. The fizz and acidity will balance the sweetness. Avoid anything too sweet or rich. For a variation on this recipe, use vanilla bean instead of cardamom and serve with passionfruit coulis.

GREEN APPLE + GINGER BEER SORBET

Ginger beer blends beautifully with the tang of green apples in this refreshing sorbet. Sometimes, a simple sorbet is all you need to complete a meal.

750g Granny Smith apples
330ml ginger beer
200g caster sugar
100g liquid glucose

SERVES 8–10
PREP 30 MINS
+ CHILLING

1 Peel and core the apples. Cut into 3cm sized pieces, put in a container and freeze for 3–4 hours.

2 Place the sugar, liquid glucose and ginger beer in a saucepan. Slowly heat through for 2 minutes until the sugar dissolves. Remove from the heat and let cool completely. Cover and refrigerate.

3 Put the frozen apples and ginger beer mixture in a blender and process until smooth. Pass through a fine sieve, then churn in an ice cream maker until the sorbet reaches desired consistency.

4 Place in a freezer-proof container and keep frozen until ready to use. Remove from the freezer a few minutes before serving.

This can be served solo or is delicious alongside some sliced apples and crumbled gingernut biscuits. If you don't have an ice cream maker, freeze the sorbet mixture in ice cube trays for a few hours. Process the iced sorbet cubes in a blender and return to the freezer until ready to serve.

OAT + NUT MACAROONS

This is my favourite macaroon recipe. Wonderful to serve at high tea parties or make gorgeous gifts during the holiday season. Use good quality vanilla and almond extracts to ensure great flavours.

- 1½ cups wholegrain oats, ground
- ¼ cup wholegrain oats for sprinkling
- 4 cups almond meal
- 1 Tbsp pistachios, ground
- ½ cup pistachios, chopped
- 4 egg whites
- 2 cups caster sugar
- 3 Tbsp pure vanilla extract
- ⅛ tsp almond extract
- 1 Tbsp butter, melted
- 1 Tbsp golden syrup

MAKES 30–40
PREP 45 MINS
COOKING 30 MINS

1. Preheat the oven to 170–180°C. Line 2 baking trays with baking paper marked with 4cm diameter circles, about 5cm apart.

2. Beat the egg whites in a bowl until soft peaks form. Gradually add the sugar, beating as you go.

3. Add the vanilla and almond extracts and continue to beat until the mixture is pale and forms a stiff peak when lifted.

4. Gradually fold the almond meal, ground pistachios and ground oats into the meringue.

5. Add the melted butter mixed with golden syrup and gently combine. Do not overmix!

6. Spoon the macaroon mixture into a piping bag and use to fill the circles you've marked out on the baking paper. Sprinkle the chopped pistachios and remaining wholegrain oats on top.

7. Bake for 20–25 minutes, or until the macaroons are lightly golden brown. Leave on the trays to cool completely. Store in an airtight container. The macaroons will keep for several weeks.

CARDAMOM + ROSE SAGO PAYASAM/ MILK PUDDING

Traditionally served at weddings and Hindu festivities, payasam is a favourite dessert for many Sri Lankans. The condensed milk sweetens the pudding without the need for any additional sugar. Cardamom adds a delightful spicy-sweet flavour and the rose water contributes a fresh floral fragrance.

¾ cup sago
¾ tsp cardamom powder, freshly ground
1½ tsp pure rose water
3½ cups water
¾ cup coconut milk or regular milk
¾–1 cup sweetened condensed milk
1 tsp butter
¼ cup cashew nut pieces
¼ cup raisins

MAKES 6–8
PREP 30 MINS
COOKING 30 MINS

1. Bring the water to a boil in a saucepan. Add the sago and cook for 10–12 minutes or until the sago pearls become translucent. Stir constantly to prevent any lumps forming.

2. Stir in the coconut or fresh milk, and the condensed milk. Continue to cook for 5–6 minutes.

3. Add the cardamom powder and rose water. Stir well to combine. Remove from the heat and set aside.

4. Melt the butter in a small frying pan and toast the cashew pieces until golden. Stir in the raisins and fry for 30–45 seconds. Remove from the heat.

5. Add the fried nuts and raisins mixture to the cooked sago pudding and stir well to combine.

6. Decorate with extra cashew nuts and raisins and serve warm in individual dishes.

GINGER MACADAMIA WAFERS

Crunchy, with an intense savoury hit from the ginger, these wafers are an excellent accompaniment to ice cream, classic crème brûlée and crème caramel desserts. They are also a treat in themselves with a cup of aromatic Ceylon tea.

10g crystallised ginger, finely chopped
1 Tbsp ground dry ginger
50g macadamia nuts, roughly chopped
2½ Tbsp butter
1½ Tbsp liquid glucose
1 egg white
⅓ cup caster sugar
¼ cup plain flour

MAKES 15–18
PREP 30 MINS
COOKING 30 MINS

1. Preheat oven to 180°C. Line a large baking tray with baking paper.

2. Place all the ingredients except the macadamia nuts in a mixing bowl and beat until smooth.

3. Using a spatula, spread the mixture thinly on the lined baking tray.

4. Sprinkle the macadamia nuts on top of the wafer mixture and bake for 15 minutes. Remove the tray from the oven.

5. Cut along the wafer to mark out the size of the pieces you wish to serve (15–18 wafers). Return to the oven for a further 15 minutes. Bake until golden.

6. Remove from the oven. While warm, lift the wafer pieces from the tray and drape them over a greased rolling pin to cool. Alternatively, cool the large wafer piece in the baking tray and break into shards. Store in an airtight container.

WALNUT CARAMEL TORTE

Walnuts are a rich source of essential fatty acids and nutrients. I adapted my mum's favourite torte recipe to include the delicious buttery-crunch of walnuts. Perfumed with orange zest and decorated with caramel icing, this torte is heaven on a plate.

60g walnuts, ground
125g walnuts halves, toasted, for sprinkling
125g caster sugar
4 eggs, separated
60g plain flour
2 tsp pure vanilla extract
½ tsp baking powder
2 Tbsp corn or canola oil
3 Tbsp boiling water
zest of 1 orange

For the caramelised white chocolate icing

100g white chocolate buttons
100ml fresh cream
2 Tbsp soft butter
80g icing sugar
1 tsp pure vanilla extract
a pinch of salt

SERVES 6–8
PREP 45 MINS
COOKING 60 MINS

1. Preheat the oven to 180°C. Lightly grease a round (21cm diameter) spring-form cake tin, dust with flour and shake off the excess.

To make the cake

2. Place the sugar, oil, egg yolks, flour, ground walnuts, vanilla and water in a bowl. Beat until the mixture becomes pale and smooth.

3. Whisk the egg whites until stiff and fold into the cake mixture. Add the orange zest and stir until combined.

4. Pour the mixture into the baking pan and bake in the centre of the oven for 30–35 minutes, or until a skewer comes out clean. Remove from the oven and cool in the tin for 15–20 minutes. Transfer the cake to a wire rack to cool completely.

To make the icing

5. Place the chocolate buttons in a glass bowl and microwave on high for 30 seconds. Stir well with a spatula and repeat this process three times, or until the chocolate begins to caramelise and release a pleasant caramel aroma. Remove, stir well again and set aside.

6. Place the cream in a saucepan and heat until bubbles appear at the edges. Stir the caramelised chocolate mixture into the cream and continue to cook over a low heat for 15–18 minutes, or until the sauce thickens considerably. Stir in the pinch of salt and remove from the heat. Set aside to cool completely.

 If you are serving this gorgeous torte for dessert, add orange segments and vanilla bean ice cream on the side.

To decorate

7 Place the butter, icing sugar and vanilla extract in a bowl and beat until the mixture is light and fluffy. Stir in the caramel sauce and beat until smooth. Spread the icing on top and around the sides of the cake.

8 Sprinkle on the walnut halves. Chop them roughly if you prefer smaller pieces.

MINI MERINGUES

Mini meringues makes a fabulous decoration and add fun textures to any dessert.

1 large egg white
50g caster sugar
¼ tsp vanilla paste

MAKES 15
PREP 30 MINS
COOKING 45 MINS

1. Preheat the oven to 100°C. Line a baking tray with baking paper.

2. Whisk the egg white in a clean bowl using an electric mixer until soft peaks form. Gradually add the sugar, 1 tsp at a time, and whisk until the mixture is glossy.

3. Add the vanilla bean paste and stir gently until combined. Spoon the mixture into a piping bag fitted with a nozzle. Pipe small blobs or stars on the lined baking tray.

4. Place the tray in the oven with the door slightly ajar. Bake for about 35–40 minutes. Turn the oven off and leave the meringues in the oven for 45 minutes. They should be dry and their outer shells firm to the touch.

5. Once cool, store the meringues in an airtight container.

For something a little different, try adding flavours to your meringues. My favourites are almond, citrus and rose.

CHOCOLATE SHARDS

If you are looking to take your dessert presentation to the next level, try these chocolate shards. They are so versatile and make an excellent accent for most plated desserts.

75g confectionary white or dark chocolate buttons

MAKES 15
PREP 30 MINS
+ SETTING
COOKING 30 MINS

1. Line a baking tray with baking paper.

2. Place the chocolate buttons in a heatproof bowl, over a saucepan of simmering water. Make sure that the water or steam doesn't come into contact with the chocolate.

3. Stir the chocolate frequently until it starts to melt. Remove from the heat and stir for 2–3 minutes.

4. Spread evenly on the lined tray, using a spatula. Let the chocolate set at room temperature or put it in the freezer for 45–50 minutes.

5. Lift the set chocolate from the tray and break into shards.

APRICOTS 3 WAYS W/ CRÈME ANGLAISE + ALMOND CAKE

This stunning dessert celebrates the arrival of golden, ripe apricots from the orchards of Central Otago. Sweet and creamy vanilla-infused custard beautifully balances the acidity of the fruit. The refreshing sorbet is spiced up with green chilli and ginger. A perfect summer treat.

For the apricot sorbet
- 500g apricots, cut into quarters, stones removed
- 45ml water, plus 125ml water
- 150g sugar
- 2 Tbsp liquid glucose
- 2cm piece fresh ginger, grated
- ½ tsp green chilli, finely chopped

For poached apricots and purée
- 275g apricots, sliced and stones removed
- zest of ½ a lemon
- 110g caster sugar
- 2 Tbsp water
- 1 vanilla pod, split

For almond cake
- 100g butter, softened
- 100g sugar
- 2 eggs
- 50g flour
- 50g ground almonds
- 1 tsp baking powder
- 1 tsp almond extract
- 75g slivered almonds

To make the sorbet
1. Place 45ml water, the sugar and liquid glucose in a saucepan and bring to a boil. Heat through for 5 minutes until the sugar is dissolved. Remove from the heat and set aside to cool down completely.

2. In a food processor, purée the apricot quarters with the ginger and 125ml water. Transfer to a large bowl with the green chilli. Whisk in the sugar syrup. Churn in an ice cream maker and transfer to a freezer-proof container and freeze overnight.

To poach the apricots
3. Place the lemon zest, sugar, water and scraped vanilla seeds with the vanilla pod into a saucepan. Bring to the boil and stir occasionally until the sugar dissolves.

4. Add the apricot slices to the hot syrup and cook for 1 minute. Remove from the heat and set aside.

To make the apricot puree
5. Place half of the poached apricots in a blender. Blend to a purée. Keep refrigerated until required. Set the other half of the poached apricots aside until ready to serve the dessert.

To make the almond cakes
6. Preheat the oven to 180°C. Place eight cupcake cases (7cm diameter, 2.5cm height) on a baking tray.

7. Beat the butter and sugar together in a bowl until the mixture is light and fluffy. Add the eggs, beating well after each addition.

For crème anglaise
2 egg yolks
50g sugar
375ml fresh cream
1 vanilla pod, split

SERVES 8
PREP 60 MINS
+ FREEZING
COOKING 30 MINS

8   In a separate bowl, mix the flour, ground almonds and baking powder. Fold into the creamed butter mixture with the almond extract. Stir to combine.

9   Spoon the mixture equally into the cupcake cases. Scatter the slivered almonds on top and bake for 15–20 minutes, or until the cakes are golden. Drizzle a little of the liquid from the remaining poached apricots over the warm cakes. Set aside.

To make the crème anglaise

10 Whisk together the egg yolks and sugar until pale and creamy.

11 In a saucepan, heat the cream with the vanilla pod and seeds until small bubbles appear around the edge. Gradually pour the hot cream over the egg mixture, whisking continuously.

12 Pour the crème anglaise back into the saucepan and gently heat for 2–3 minutes, or until it is thick enough to coat the back of a spoon.

13 Serve the almond cake with a quenelle of apricot sorbet, crème anglaise, the rest of the poached apricot slices and the apricot purée.

BOYSENBERRY TRIFLE

This boysenberry trifle is a quintessentially summer treat. I love using glass goblets to show off the contrasting layers. Absolutely decadent and visually appealing, this pudding can be prepared in advance for a dinner party or special occasion.

For the soaking liquid and boysenberry jelly
350g boysenberries
4 Tbsp sugar
500ml water
2 gelatine leaves

For the whisked sponge
2 eggs
50g caster sugar
50g plain flour

To make the soaking liquid

1 Place the sugar and water in a saucepan and heat through to dissolve the sugar. Add the berries and gently poach for 4–5 minutes. Remove from the heat, mash the softened berries and pass through a fine sieve into a bowl.

2 Divide the berry syrup in half. Set the first half aside to cool at room temperature. Then store in the fridge until needed. Use the other half immediately to make the boysenberry jelly.

To make the jelly

3 Soak the gelatine leaves in a bowl of cold water for a few minutes.

4 Take the gelatine leaves from the water and wring gently to remove excess water. Add to the hot berry syrup and whisk to combine. Cool at room temperature. Refrigerate until the jelly is set firm.

To make the sponge

5 Preheat the oven to 180°C. Lightly grease a round, 21cm spring-form cake tin, dust with flour and shake off the excess.

6 Place the egg yolks and sugar in a bowl over a pan of simmering water. Beat with an electric mixer until light and foamy. Remove the bowl from the pan and continue to whisk until the mixture cools down.

7 Sift the flour and fold it into the egg mixture, a little at a time until combined. Pour into the prepared cake tin and bake for 12–15 minutes, or until the sponge starts to peel away from the side of the tin. Cool slightly in the tin before turning out onto a wire rack.

Continued over page

For the vanilla custard
1 vanilla pod
200ml fresh cream
75ml full cream milk
2 large egg yolks
50g caster sugar
1 Tbsp cornflour

For the Chantilly cream
200ml fresh cream
3 tsp icing sugar
the seeds of 1 vanilla pod

SERVES 4–5
PREP 45 MINS
+ SETTING
COOKING 30 MINS

To make the custard
8. Split the vanilla pod lengthwise and scrape out the seeds. Place the pod and seeds in a saucepan with the cream and milk. As soon as the mixture begins to boil, remove from the heat.

9. Whisk the egg yolks, cornflour, and sugar in a bowl until pale and thick. Gradually add the hot cream mixture, continually whisking until combined.

10. Pour this mixture back into the saucepan and stir over low heat until the custard thickens and coats the back of the spoon. Remove from the heat and pass through a sieve into a bowl. Set aside to cool. Refrigerate until required.

To make the Chantilly cream
11. Whisk all ingredients together until soft peaks form.

To serve
12. Cut the sponge into 1.5cm pieces and place in the bottom of each serving goblet. Drizzle the boysenberry soaking liquid over the sponge.

13. Spoon small blobs of set jelly over the soaked sponge. Pour the chilled custard over the jelly. Pipe the Chantilly cream on top. Finish with a few fresh boysenberries.

A sweeter style of Sparkling Rosé, like Brachetto d'Acqui will match nicely, balancing the creaminess and the tartness of this dessert.

DECONSTRUCTED RASPBERRY + WHITE CHOCOLATE CHEESECAKE W/ LYCHEE SORBET

This decadent deconstructed cheesecake was designed with a special occasion dinner party in mind. The classic combination of white chocolate and raspberry is paired with refreshingly fragrant lychee sorbet and crunchy hazelnut crumbs. None of the elements is too laborious to make and when artistically presented, they combine to create an impressive dessert.

For the lychee sorbet
565g canned lychees in syrup
2 Tbsp caster sugar
2 Tbsp water
2 Tbsp liquid glucose
juice of 1 lime
½ tsp rose water
pink colouring (optional)

For the raspberry coulis
200g raspberries
100g caster sugar
1 Tbsp of water

For the hazelnut crumbs
50g caster sugar
50g flour
50g hazelnuts, ground
50g butter

To make the lychee sorbet
1. Place the sugar in a saucepan with the water and liquid glucose. Gently heat the mixture for 2–3 minutes until the sugar dissolves. Remove from the heat and cool completely.

2. Mix the sugar syrup with the lychees, lime juice, rose water and pink colouring. Process in a blender until smooth. Churn this mixture in an ice cream maker until the sorbet reaches desired consistency. Transfer to a freezer-proof container and freeze for 6–8 hours. Remove from the freezer a few minutes before serving.

To make the coulis
3. Place the raspberries, water and sugar in a saucepan and gently heat until the sugar dissolves. Let simmer for 1–2 minutes. Blend in a food processor and strain the mixture through a fine sieve. Set aside until required.

To make the hazelnut crumbs
4. Preheat the oven to 180°C. Line a baking tray with baking paper.

5. Combine the dry ingredients in a bowl. Rub in the butter until incorporated. Spread the mixture on the lined baking tray and bake for 15–20 minutes, or until golden brown. Remove from the oven and set aside to cool. Using a rolling pin, crush into crumbs. Store in an airtight container until required.

Continued over page

For the cheesecake filling

50g white chocolate buttons
1 vanilla pod
250g cream cheese
250g thickened cream
45g icing sugar

For the decoration

12–15 raspberries
250g lychees in syrup, drained
white chocolate shards*
*Refer to recipe on page 329

SERVES 8
PREP 60 MINS
+ FREEZING
COOKING 30 MINS

To make the cheesecake filling

6 Split the vanilla pod, scrape out the seeds and place them in a bowl with the white chocolate buttons. Gently melt the chocolate over a saucepan of simmering water. Remove the bowl from the heat and set aside to cool.

7 In a separate bowl, place the cream cheese, icing sugar, and thickened cream. Add the melted chocolate and whip until the mixture is thoroughly combined. Transfer to a large piping bag and refrigerate for 25–30 minutes.

To serve

8 Brush each serving plate with raspberry coulis. Pipe on three round dollops of cheesecake filling. Sprinkle the golden hazelnut crumbs around the cheesecake dollops and finish with extra lychees, fresh raspberries and white chocolate shards. Spoon on a quenelle of lychee sorbet and serve.

If you don't have an ice cream maker, freeze the sorbet mixture in ice cube trays for a few hours. Process the iced sorbet cubes in a blender and return to the freezer until ready to serve.

CHOCOLATE CAKE

Whatever the occasion, my family celebrates special moments with this incredibly versatile cake. My precious grandchildren Ava and Leon are the latest fans. Ava has also been known to get stuck in with the baking!

500g caster sugar
500g soft butter
8 eggs, separated
375g flour
125g cocoa powder
5 tsp baking powder
½ tsp baking soda
½ tsp cream of tartar
250ml milk
4 tsp pure vanilla extract

For the icing
275g soft butter
500g icing sugar, sifted
100g cocoa powder, sifted
2 tsp pure vanilla extract
1 Tbsp boiling water

SERVES 10–12
PREP 45 MINS
COOKING 45 MINS

1. Preheat the oven to 180°C. Grease two cake tins (25cm diameter) and line with baking paper.

2. Beat the sugar and butter until pale and creamy. Add the egg yolks one at a time, beating well after each addition. Set aside.

3. In a separate bowl, whip the egg whites to stiff peaks.

4. **In a separate bowl,** sift together the flour, cocoa, baking soda, baking powder and cream of tartar.

5. Alternating between the dry ingredients, the egg whites and the milk, gradually fold them into the butter mixture. Add the vanilla extract and stir gently until combined.

6. Pour the mixture into the prepared cake tins and bake for 38–45 minutes or until a skewer comes out clean. Remove from the oven and cool on a wire rack.

To make the chocolate icing

7. Beat the butter until light and creamy. Add the icing sugar, cocoa, vanilla extract and boiling water and beat until the mixture is light and fluffy.

8. Spread the icing over one cake. Place the second cake on top. Decorate with the remaining icing as desired.

DARK CHOCOLATE MOUSSE CAKES W/ ORANGE LIQUEUR CREAM

Smooth, velvety and fabulously delicious, these individual chocolate desserts can tempt anyone, whether they have a sweet tooth or not. Raspberry and kiwifruit sauces add a luxurious touch to this indulgent dessert.

For the orange vanilla sponge
1 egg
75g caster sugar
2 Tbsp fresh cream
75g self-raising flour
1/8 tsp baking powder
25g butter, melted
1 tsp pure vanilla extract
zest of one orange

For the chocolate mousse
200g dark chocolate (70% cocoa)
2 whole eggs
2-3 Tbsp caster sugar
2 Tbsp water
300ml fresh cream
½ tsp gelatine, dissolved in 1 Tbsp warm water

To make the sponge
1. Preheat the oven to 180°C. Place the egg and sugar in a bowl. Beat until light and fluffy. Stir in the cream until combined.

2. **In a separate bowl**, sift together the flour and baking powder. Add the orange zest and fold into the egg mixture. Add the melted butter and vanilla extract, stirring gently until combined.

3. Line a cake tin (20cm x 20cm) with baking paper. Spoon in the sponge cake batter and bake for 14–15 minutes, until lightly golden and springy to the touch. Set aside to cool. Cut the sponge into 8cm diameter circles.

To form the base of the desserts
4. Arrange 6 serving rings (8cm diameter) on a baking tray lined with baking paper. Cut 4 strips of baking paper (30cm x 12cm). Twist each into a collar and place inside each of serving rings.

5. Transfer the cut cake rounds into prepared serving rings, push down firmly and chill in the refrigerator.

To make the mousse
6. Place the chocolate in a heatproof bowl over a saucepan of simmering water and stir until melted and smooth. Set aside to cool.

7. Place the eggs in a bowl and whisk until pale and creamy.

Continued over page

For the orange liqueur cream
250ml fresh cream, whipped
2–3 tsp orange liqueur (e.g. Cointreau)

For the sauces
1 cup raspberries
2 kiwi fruits, peeled and diced
4 Tbsp caster sugar
green food colouring (optional)

For the garnish
1 Tbsp pistachios, ground coarsely
chocolate decorations (optional)

SERVES 6
PREP 60 MINS
COOKING 30 MINS

8. In a saucepan, bring the sugar and water to a boil. Slowly pour this hot syrup into the beaten eggs, whisking continuously. Let the mixture cool completely.

9. Gently fold the melted chocolate into the egg mixture.

10. In a separate bowl, whip the cream until soft peaks form. Combine the dissolved gelatine with the cream and gently fold into the chocolate-egg mixture. Spoon this mixture over the prepared cake bases in the serving rings. Refrigerate for 6–8 hours until firm.

To make the orange liqueur cream
11. Mix the whipped cream with the orange liqueur in a bowl. Cover and keep refrigerated until required.

To make the raspberry sauce
12. In a blender, purée the raspberries with 2 Tbsp of sugar. Pass through a sieve into a bowl, cover and refrigerate.

To make the kiwifruit sauce
13. In a blender, purée the kiwifruit with the remaining 2 Tbsp of sugar. Pass through a sieve into a bowl, cover and refrigerate. For a bright green sauce, add one or two drops of green food colouring.

To serve
14. Remove the paper collars and serving rings and transfer the mousse cakes onto individual serving plates. Decorate with orange liqueur cream, chocolate decorations, ground pistachios and the fruit sauces. Serve chilled.

To bring out the orange flavour in the cream, try this with Madeira, which has nice orange peel notes.

LOVE HEARTS WITH BERRY COULIS, PAGE 348.

LOVE HEARTS W/ BERRY COULIS

I created these heart-shaped desserts with Valentine's Day in mind. Inside an elegant chocolate shell sits a velvet caramel mousse with a fluid berry centre. The hearts are surrounded by crème patissiere and berry coulis. What else can declare love better than chocolate and bright summer berries?

For the chocolate cases
250g dark chocolate melts/buttons

For the berry coulis
150g fresh raspberries
150g fresh strawberries, hulled
30g icing sugar

For the caramelised white chocolate mousse filling
1 Tbsp caster sugar
1 Tbsp water
200ml fresh cream
100g white chocolate buttons
1 egg
¾ tsp gelatine mixed with ½ Tbsp warm water
½ tsp caramel flavouring

1. You will need 4 heart-shaped silicone moulds (100ml capacity) and mini dome moulds (5ml capacity) for the berry filling inside the chocolate hearts. The hearts and filling can be prepared in advance and assembled on the day.

To make the berry coulis

2. Blend the berries with icing sugar and pass through a sieve. Transfer the coulis into a squeeze bottle.

3. Fill the mini dome moulds with berry coulis and place in the freezer to solidify. Keep any remaining coulis in the fridge until required.

To make the chocolate heart cases

4. Melt chocolate buttons in a heatproof bowl, over a saucepan of simmering water.

5. Coat each heart mould base evenly with melted chocolate to form a heart-shaped chocolate shell. You may need to do a few layers of chocolate coating to ensure even thickness. Be sure to make a few extra in case of breakages.

To make the mousse filling

6. Place the white chocolate buttons in a glass bowl and microwave on high at 30 second intervals.

7. Stir well with a spatula after each interval and continue this process a few times until the chocolate begins to caramelise and release a pleasant caramel aroma.

8. Remove from the microwave, stir thoroughly and set aside.

For the crème patissiere
250ml full cream milk
50g caster sugar
1 vanilla pod
3 egg yolks
1 Tbsp plain flour
1 Tbsp cornflour
100ml pouring cream

For the decoration
15–20 fresh strawberries
sugar spun decorations (optional)

MAKES 4
PREP 75 MINS
+SETTING
COOKING 30 MINS

9 Place 50ml of the cream in a saucepan and heat until bubbles appear at the edge. Add the caramelised chocolate mixture. Stir and continue to cook over low heat for 8–10 minutes, or until the sauce thickens considerably. Remove from the heat and set aside to cool.

10 Place the egg in a bowl and whisk until pale and creamy.

11 In a saucepan, bring the sugar and water to a boil. Slowly pour this hot syrup into the beaten egg, whisking continuously until the mixture cools completely.

12 Whip the remaining 150ml of cream in a separate bowl until soft peaks form. Add the dissolved gelatine to the whipped cream. Lightly fold the cream mixture into the egg mixture.

13 Add the cooled caramelised white chocolate sauce and stir well to combine. Fill a piping bag with the mousse and refrigerate for 2–3 hours.

To make the crème patissiere

14 Place the egg yolks with the sugar in a bowl. Using an electric beater, whisk until light and creamy. Stir in the flour and cornflour and beat until combined.

15 Split the vanilla pod in half and carefully scrape out the seeds with a sharp knife. Place the vanilla seeds and pod in a saucepan. Add the milk and bring it to the boil gradually. Remove from the heat as soon as the milk starts to bubble around the edge.

16 Pour the warm milk gradually into the egg mixture and continue to whisk. Transfer this mixture back into the saucepan and stir over a low-medium heat until the mixture thickens such that it coats the back of a spoon. Remove from the heat and transfer to a bowl. Cover with cling wrap and set aside to cool.

Continued over page.

17 Whip the pouring cream lightly and carefully fold into the crème patissiere mixture. Spoon the crème patissiere into a piping bag fitted with a nozzle. Refrigerate until required.

To assemble

18 Pipe the mousse into the prepared chocolate-covered moulds. Carefully unmould the berry centres from the mini dome moulds and press into each mousse. Top up with extra mousse to seal the berry centre inside the chocolate heart. Return to the freezer to set.

19 Line a tray with baking paper. Carefully remove the chocolate hearts from the moulds and turn out onto the lined tray. Return to the fridge until required.

To serve

20 Pipe the crème patissiere onto the plate and surround with extra berry coulis. Carefully place the chocolate hearts on top using a spatula. Decorate with spun sugar and fresh strawberry halves if desired.

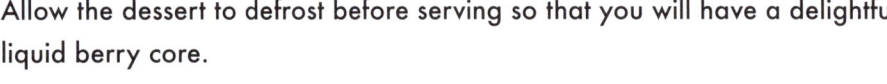

Allow the dessert to defrost before serving so that you will have a delightful liquid berry core.

DINNER PARTY MENUS

EACH SEASON OFFERS UP
ITS WONDERFUL VARIETY OF
PRODUCE.

HERE IS A COLLECTION OF
DINNER PARTY MENUS FOR THE
FOUR SEASONS.

THE COURSES ARE DESIGNED TO
COMPLEMENT ONE ANOTHER
AND TAKE YOUR GUESTS ON AN
EXCITING CULINARY JOURNEY.

IMPRESS YOUR GUESTS

1.

This menu utilises spring lamb and hapuka fish, which reach their peak availability in New Zealand during the spring season. I picked a decadent walnut torte for dessert because it can be made in advance. Orange segments bring a refreshing tartness to the sweet course.

UP TO 15 PEOPLE

Short eat/canapé
Hapuka fish cutlets (page 66)

Starter
Fish soup with coconut milk and coriander (page 142)

Main Course
Lamb leg roast with harissa and roasted garlic and yoghurt dressing (page 112)
Zesty lemony couscous (page 110)
Minty salsa (page 110)
Garden salad

Dessert
Walnut caramel torte with vanilla bean ice cream and orange segments (page 326)

2.

Lamb is the fare of New Zealand's spring. Enjoy a main course that celebrates this beautiful meat in a curry cooked with an elaborate blend of aromatic spices. If you're feeling adventurous, try the amuse-bouche course of salmon sashimi.

UP TO 10 PEOPLE

Short eat/canapé
Sambal and goat cheese mini tartlets (page 69)

Amuse-bouche
King salmon sashimi with soy miso dressing (opposite page)

Starter
Garlic prawns with avocado salsa (page 90)

Main Course
Spring lamb curry (page 202)
Eggplant white curry (page 242)
Atcharu/mixed pickle (page 283)
Tomato with coconut lime dressing (page 175)
Basmati rice

Dessert
Love Cake tartlets with orange sorbet (page 308)

For the sashimi
450g sushi-grade salmon
2 tsp extra virgin olive oil

For the dressing
3 Thai red chillies, finely sliced
1 Tbsp white miso paste
½ cup thick, sweet variety soy sauce
½ cup regular soy sauce
2 Tbsp ginger, finely grated with juices
1 Tbsp coriander leaves and stems, finely chopped
juice of 1 lemon
1 tsp rice wine vinegar
½ tsp sesame oil

To make the dressing
1. Place the ingredients in a jar and shake well to combine.

To prepare the sashimi
2. Pin bone and slice the salmon into 3mm thick strips. Lightly coat with the oil. Arrange across a serving platter. Serve immediately with the soy-miso dressing on the side for dipping.

3.

Juicy prawns paired with mango relish is a perfect canapé, bringing texture and sour fruitiness. My fish starter introduces umami flavours. The stunning apricot dessert with a spiced sorbet cleanses the palate, following the main meal of rich duck leg. This menu features vibrant dishes and heavenly combinations that highlight the best of summer.

UP TO 15 PEOPLE

Short eat/canapé
Avocado and prawn crostini with mango relish (page 72)

Starter
Panko crusted fish with spicy miso broth (page 135)

Main Course
Szechuan duck legs with coconut milk rice (page 114)

Dessert
Apricots 3 ways with crème anglaise and almond cake (page 333)

4.

Subtly spiced crispy masala vadai sets a sassy tone for this menu. A Moroccan tagine-style venison dish swings away from the traditional Sri Lankan flavours and an energising summer sorbet ends the meal.

UP TO 10 PEOPLE

Short eat/canapé
Masala vadai (page 81)

Starter
Scallops with tangy cherry sauce (page 85)

Main Course
Tagine-style venison (page 126)
Brinjal/eggplant pickle (page 280)
Chickpeas with spinach and red peppers (page 243)
Saffron pilaf rice (opposite page)
Roti (page 52)

Dessert
Green apple and ginger beer sorbet (page 321)
Ginger macadamia wafers (page 325)

3 cups basmati rice
2 cups chicken or vegetable stock
2 pink shallots, sliced
5cm piece cinnamon stick
2 cloves
4 cardamom pods
½ tsp saffron
salt to taste
15g butter
1 Tbsp butter
1 Tbsp pistachio nuts
2 Tbsp dried cranberries
½ cup coriander leaves, chopped

1. Wash the rice thoroughly and drain in a colander.

2. Soak the saffron threads in 2 Tbsp of warm water. Heat the butter in a frying pan. Add the sliced shallots, cinnamon stick, cardamom, cloves and gently fry for 30–45 seconds until fragrant.

3. Transfer the rice mix into a rice cooker with the salt, chicken stock and soaked saffron with its liquid. Cook.

4. Melt the butter in a frying pan and gently fry the pistachios and cranberries. Mix in with the cooked rice.

5. Garnish with coriander leaves and serve.

5.

This menu is designed for vegetarians and features some of my favourite recipes. From sweet onion tartlets to lavish rice and curry combinations, this dinner party menu is sure to impress your vegetarian guests, as well as the meat lovers.

UP TO 10 PEOPLE

Short eat/canapé
Sri Lankan caramelised onion tarlets (page 69, remove the anchovies)

Starter
Sweet potato soup with zingy coriander pesto and garlic butter baguette (opposite page)

Main Course
Sambar (page 250)
Potato masala (page 254)
Fried eggplant curry (page 260)
Coconut sambal (page 272)
Dosa (page 46)

Dessert
Chocolate cake (page 342)

500g sweet potato, diced into 1cm cubes
1 onion, finely diced
5cm fresh ginger, grated
3cm piece of fresh turmeric, grated
½ cup coconut milk
5 cups vegetable stock
juice of 1 lime
2 cloves of garlic, crushed
2 tbsp oil
salt to taste

For the coriander pesto
1 cup fresh coriander leaves
1 Tbsp mint leaves
1 clove of garlic
1–2 green chillies
2 Tbsp cashew nuts, toasted
¼ cup light olive oil
juice of ½ a lime
salt to taste

For garnish
4–5 tbsp coconut cream
coriander leaves

To make the soup

1. Heat the oil in a large pan. Sauté the onion, turmeric, and ginger for 3–4 minutes over a low heat until soft and lightly caramelised.

2. Add the diced sweet potato with salt and sauté for 4–5 minutes.

3. Add the stock and bring it to a boil. Cook for 8–10 minutes or until the sweet potato is soft and cooked through.

4. Add the coconut milk, crushed garlic and remove from the heat. Blend with a stick blender until smooth. Add the lime juice.

To make the pesto

5. Place all the ingredients in a food processor and process coarsely. Refrigerate until ready to serve.

To serve

6. Ladle the soup into individual bowls, add a swirl of coconut cream and a spoonful of coriander pesto in the middle. Garnish with coriander leaves.

6.

Start with spicy venison pasties, followed by refreshing tabbouleh, which cleanses the palate. Then, wow your guests further with crayfish topped with herb butter. Crispy wafer-thin Sri Lankan egg hoppers are served with a variety of spicy curries. Finish the meal with the sweet notes of orange-infused crème caramel.

UP TO 15 PEOPLE

Short eat/canapé
Venison pasties (page 78)

Amuse-bouche
Quinoa tabbouleh with pomegranate seeds (page 193)

Starter
Herb butter crayfish (page 132)
Jerusalem artichoke purée (opposite page)
Pickled vegetables (opposite page)

Main Course
Jaffna chicken curry (page 225)
Beetroot curry (page 246)
Tomato chutney (page 285)
Coconut sambal (page 272)
Egg hopper (page 48)

Dessert
Orange-infused crème caramel (page 310)

For the artichoke purée

500g Jerusalem artichokes, sliced
300ml thickened cream
salt to taste
freshly ground black pepper

For the pickle

450gm carrots
450gm daikon or white radish
2cm ginger, julienned
150gm caster sugar
salt to taste
2 cups of white vinegar
2 cups of water
½ tsp mustard seeds

To make the purée

1 Place artichokes in a saucepan and add enough water to cover. Simmer until the artichokes are tender.

2 Once the artichokes are cooked, drain and place back in the pan with the cream and salt. Bring to the boil and simmer for 5–6 minutes. Add freshly ground pepper and blend until smooth. Keep warm until required.

To make the pickle

3 Wash, peel and cut the pickling vegetables into 0.75cm x 6cm long batons. Place the water in a saucepan with the sugar, vinegar, mustard seeds and ginger. Bring to a boil.

4 Add the carrots and daikon to the pickling mixture and heat for 30–60 seconds. Pack tightly into a pickling jar and seal. Once cool, refrigerate until required.

7.

Crab cakes are delicately spiced and infused with fresh herbs while the mango chilli aioli adds layers of spicy, tangy flavours in this autumnal menu. Highly aromatic lamb biriyani brings big Indian flavours to the main meal. Make your panna cotta in clear glasses to show off the colourful layers!

UP TO 10 PEOPLE

Short eat/canapé
Crab cakes with mango chilli aioli (page 68)

Amuse-bouche
Chickpea pakoda (page 130)

Main Course
Lamb biriyani (page 206, substitute the chicken for lamb leg)
Egg and red onion salad (page 174)

Dessert
Cardamom panna cotta with raspberry-rose jelly and spiced biscuits (page 318)